RAISING DOUGH FOR
# Marymount
A CORK COOKBOOK

*Gary Burke*

Photography by
Fionn Mulvey

MERCIER PRESS

# CONTENTS

## BAKER'S CORNER

Sutton's scones with sweet cream
& fresh strawberries 21

Sutton's brown bread 22

White soda bread 25

Rocket, sun-dried tomato &
mozzarella loaf 26

Walnut & banana bread 29

Tea cake with brandy icing 30

Rosemary, tomato & green olive focaccia 33

Roco's quiche 34

Olive oil & lemon verbena cake 37

Gluten-free chocolate & orange cake 38

The Burkes' Christmas cake 41

## STARTERS

Crock of Glenbeigh mussels 46

Crispy tempura of vegetables 49

Chilli beef & baby gem wraps, blue
cheese & toasted cashew nuts 50

Duck pastilla roll with
roasted plums & guacamole 53

Chicken-liver parfait with
fig & apple chutney 56

Buffalo mozzarella, chargrilled
vegetables & rocket pesto bruschetta 58

Carrigtwohill baked potatoes 61

Posh sausage roll with home-made
ketchup 64

Prawns pil-pil with raita &
black olive toasted loaf 66

'Saturday night nachos' 69

Ted's smoked haddock fishcakes with
sweetcorn purée, red pepper
aioli and crispy capers 72

Timoleague sticky pork ribs 74

Castletownbere scallops, pancetta &
garden peas with pea cream 77

## STARTERS

| | |
|---|---|
| Roco's superfood salad | 78 |
| West Cork BBQ beef salad with Franciscan Well beer dressing | 82 |
| Pasta caprese rigatoni with plum tomatoes & buffalo mozzarella | 84 |
| Lemon & thyme roasted chicken, cherry tomato, mango, Parmesan shavings & lime & chilli yoghurt | 87 |
| Sticky teriyaki chicken with mango & coriander salsa & beansprout salad | 88 |
| Goats' cheese, beetroot & green bean salad | 91 |
| Vegetable & barley broth | 92 |
| Spicy carrot & lentil soup | 95 |
| Chicken & noodle soup | 96 |
| Ballycotton chunky seafood chowder | 99 |
| Roast red pepper & tomato soup with cheese croutons | 100 |
| Pumpkin soup with fresh sage & toasted pumpkin seeds | 103 |

## MAIN COURSES

| | |
|---|---|
| Dad's bacon & cabbage | 108 |
| The Corkonian beef burger with Gubbeen cheese, fat fries & pink sauce | 112 |
| Fried buttermilk chicken strips with crispy sweet potato cubes & a roast garlic aioli | 116 |
| Pot-roasted Midleton lamb shank with spiced red cabbage, honey-roasted carrots & mint sauce | 120 |
| Spicy vegetable lasagne with goats' cheese toasties | 124 |
| Grilled salmon fillet with pumpkin seed & sun-dried tomato crust, squash purée & braised baby potatoes | 128 |
| Cottage pie with smoked Applewood cheddar mash | 130 |
| Chicken curry | 133 |
| Blackened turkey tacos, tomato & bean salsa, avocado & sour cream | 134 |
| Beef short rib in red wine with roast garlic mash & pickled onion sauce | 138 |

## MAIN COURSES

Clonakilty chicken supreme with sweetcorn
purée, sprouting broccoli & crushed baby
potatoes                                        141

Monkfish scampi, pea purée,
lemon aioli & pea shoots                         142

Honey-roasted Skeaghanore West Cork
duck breast, root vegetable salad, pearl
barley & blackcurrant sauce                      146

Hake fillet, cannellini bean, tomato &
chorizo stew with lime crème fraîche             148

Pan-fried fillet steak with baby spinach,
forest mushrooms, onion jam &
tarragon butter                                  152

Whole roast sea bass with red chilli, roasted
sweet potato wedges & spring onion &
caper salsa                                      155

The Burkes' Christmas dinner
with all the trimmings                           158

Christy's corned-beef hash
with poached egg, mustard mayo
& rocket & tomato salad                          162

## DESSERTS

Gerry's chocolate pots with
shortbread biscuits                              166

The Mahon knickerbocker glory                    169

Banana tarte Tatin with crispy
almonds & mascarpone cream                       170

Lemon posset with crisp honeycomb &
roasted strawberries                             173

Kamil's mango cheesecake
with passion fruit                               176

Mini Pavlova with fresh fruit
& lemon curd                                     179

Raspberry millefeuille                           180

Sticky toffee pudding with
vanilla ice cream & toffee sauce                 183

Chocolate & strawberry trifle                    184

Apple madeira with fresh berries
& caramel sauce                                  187

Lemon tart with fresh
raspberries & raspberry purée                    188

Chocolate soufflé with
Jameson anglaise                                 191

Mixed berry & pear crumble with custard          192

# KIDS

In providing excellent care,
we cherish the uniqueness and
dignity of each person, showing
compassion and respect. We strive
for quality and integrity in all we do.

Marymount's mission statement

# A SHORT HISTORY OF MARYMOUNT

Marymount University Hospital and Hospice owes its origins to the inspiration of Dr Patrick Murphy, who, from his own experiences living and working in Cork, was well aware of the medical needs of the sick and poor of the city. He had been impressed with the work of the Religious Sisters of Charity in Cork, founded by Mary Aikenhead, especially during the Famine. When he died in 1867, he bequeathed to the Sisters whatever remained of his estate on condition that they establish a hospital for cancer patients in Cork within two years.

On 8 May 1869 the foundation stone was laid on the site of the new hospital at Wellington Road. Because no architect was employed, the project went massively over budget and the Sisters of Charity had to add an additional sum of £1,000 so that building might proceed. The first patient to be treated at the hospital, on 29 September 1870, was Catherine Hackett.

By the beginning of the twentieth century, seven wards were in use, funded largely by church collections, donations and money left by patients in their wills. On the centenary of Sister Mary Aikenhead's death, in 1958, 100 poor men were invited to dinner. A substantial meal of bacon, cabbage and potatoes was followed by a dessert of pudding and custard, all washed down with a bottle of stout. Between 1966 and 1967 alone, the meals-on-wheels service that the nuns provided served in excess of 7,000 meals to old-age pensioners throughout the city.

Marymount Hospital and Hospice, as part of St Patrick's Hospital, was officially opened on 26 April 1984. In September 2011 Marymount moved from its long-time city-centre location to a new, purpose-built, state-of-the-art facility at Curraheen on the edge of Cork city. This provides two distinct services. The elderly care facility offers respite care, intermediate palliative care and continuing care for older people. Marymount Hospice provides care to patients with progressive illnesses, both cancer and non-cancer, at a time when pain or other symptom issues need addressing. Patients on active treatment may benefit from a short-term admission for symptom control and rehabilitation. Support is also offered to families facing loss or who are bereaved.

Marymount is the designated Specialist Care Centre for the Cork/Kerry region, serving a population of approximately 600,000. The cost of providing this service is met by a combination of state funding and, increasingly, by donated funds. By buying this cookbook you are supporting this vital and life-affirming service.

*Michael Lenihan*

# INTRODUCTION

When I was growing up, food was not important in our family. We lived in a council house in Mahon and we didn't have the money for eating out in good restaurants, but don't think I'm not proud of my upbringing. Dad and Mam worked their asses off to provide for their five young kids. We ate good, basic food and we were never hungry going to bed.

Dad used to be a chef in the army and when Mam was on shift work, Dad was on cooking duty. I would dread his cooking some days – sorry Dad! Fried liver with lumpy mash was his speciality and my stomach would be turning before I'd even sat down at the table. In our house, however, you could not leave the table unless you finished, so you had no choice but to eat up. And despite the cuisine on offer, I still cherish the memory of those meals.

Dad was always hugely supportive of me. When I decided to leave school at fifteen, after my Junior Cert, he backed me all the way. He knew that I just wanted to get into a trade and work, so he let me leave. The only catch was I had to get a job straight away, otherwise I was going back to school. That was the deal.

Sixteen was the minimum age for most trades, but luckily a commis chef position came up in Rochestown Park Hotel, so I went for an interview and I got the job. Now my idea at the time was 'two months in here and I'm gone'. I remember putting on the chef pants and thinking, if any of my friends see me I'll be an absolute laughing stock. The blue pants with tiny squares? The neck tie and the tall paper hat? The state of me!

Little did I know that I was about to start a culinary journey which would take me to the Park Hotel in Kenmare (twice), the Woodstock Hotel in Ennis, the Dunbrody House and Cookery School, a food franchise in Arklow and right back to the Rochestown Park Hotel, where today I'm the Executive Chef – a twenty-year journey there and back.

It was during my second stint at the Park in Kenmare that Dad became seriously ill. The speed with which things moved from diagnosis to Dad's passing was frightening – no more than a week. He received palliative care from the Marymount staff, who made his final journey as comfortable as possible. It is this comfort and care that Marymount is renowned for, and it was so appreciated by our family. Dad's dying wish was granted and in December 2004 he spent his final hours in his own home, surrounded by his wife and children, those he loved the most. I will always be grateful to the Marymount staff for facilitating this with such care and compassion.

I never thought I would have an opportunity to pay Marymount back for their support and care for us and for other families. I hope the money raised from this book can go some way towards repaying that debt and allow Marymount to continue offering the amazing support and services they provide. Marymount is a safe,

> "
> To help people in need is something I'm very proud of and I know that Dad would be proud too.
> "

calm environment that allows families to share those last precious moments with their loved ones.

This book is for everyone who loves food and wants to get more out of their family time and cooking. Cooking is a fun, loving and light-hearted thing to do. There is no need to get stressed, as many people do, although to be fair I've had my moments too! Ultimately, though, my work is my joy; it's my life; it keeps me happy. Who else can say they truly love what they do?

For me, writing this book has brought me joy and happiness. To be able to support Marymount in continuing to help people in need is something I'm very proud of and I know that Dad would be proud too.

Above all else, I hope this book will help you to put on an apron and cook.

Enjoy!

The Cork Chef
Raising Dough for Marymount

# TEMPERATURE CONVERSION TABLE

All oven temperatures given are in Celsius and are for fan-assisted ovens.
Below are the equivalent temperatures for conventional, gas and Fahrenheit ovens.

| Fan Oven Celsius | Conventional Oven | Gas Mark | Fahrenheit |
| --- | --- | --- | --- |
| 90°C (Very cool) | 110°C | $\frac{1}{4}$ | 225°F |
| 110°C | 130°C | $\frac{1}{2}$ | 266°F |
| 120°C (Cool) | 140°C | 1 | 275°F |
| 130°C | 150°C | 2 | 300°F |
| 140°C (Moderate) | 160°C | 3 | 325°F |
| 150°C | 170°C | 3 | 325°F |
| 160°C | 180°C | 4 | 350°F |
| 170°C (Mod. Hot) | 190°C | 5 | 375°F |
| 180°C | 200°C | 6 | 400°F |
| 190°C | 210°C | 6 | 400°F |
| 200°C (Hot) | 220°C | 7 | 425°F |
| 210°C | 230°C | 8 | 450°F |
| 220°C (Very Hot) | 240°C | 9 | 475°F |

BAKER'S CORNER

# SUTTON'S SCONES WITH SWEET CREAM & FRESH STRAWBERRIES

MAKES 10

## INGREDIENTS

560g plain flour

4g salt

6g baking powder

140g caster sugar

270g soft butter

80g golden raisins

2 large eggs, plus 1 (beaten) for glaze

80g buttermilk

Zest of 1 orange

1 tbsp milk

Icing sugar, to dust

Fresh strawberries to garnish

SWEET CREAM

200ml cream, whipped

1 tsp icing sugar

½ tsp vanilla essence

## METHOD

Preheat the oven to 170°C. Sieve the flour, salt and baking powder together. Add the sugar and then rub in the butter until it resembles fine breadcrumbs.

Add the raisins, 2 eggs, the buttermilk and the orange zest, and mix until a nice workable dough has come together.

Place onto a floured surface and gently knead the dough, then shape into a round. With a rolling pin, roll out lightly to about 25 mm in thickness. Cut the scones out with a round 7 cm cutter and place on a greased baking tray.

Brush each scone with beaten egg and milk, then bake for approximately 23 minutes until well risen and golden brown. Dust with icing sugar before serving.

For the sweet cream, whisk the cream and the icing sugar together until thick. Then mix in the vanilla essence. Serve the cream on the side garnished with the fresh strawberries.

# SUTTON'S BROWN BREAD

MAKES 1 LOAF

## INGREDIENTS

125g strong flour

295g wholemeal flour

100g plain flour

50g brown sugar

10g salt

17g bread soda

45g soft butter

600ml buttermilk

1 tsp porridge oats

## METHOD

Preheat the oven to 175°C.

Combine all the dry ingredients, excluding the oats. Then add the butter, followed by the buttermilk and mix well to form a wet dough.

Place the mixture into a 1kg greased loaf tin. Give the tin a bang on the bottom so the mixture sinks evenly.

Sprinkle the porridge oats over the top and bake for 45 minutes. Then remove the loaf from the tin, return it to the oven and bake for another 10 minutes. When the bread is fully cooked, it will sound hollow when you tap the bottom. Cool on a wire rack.

# WHITE SODA BREAD

## INGREDIENTS

450g plain flour
1 tsp baking powder
1 tsp salt
400ml buttermilk

## METHOD

Preheat the oven to 180°C.

Mix the flour, baking powder and salt together. Add the buttermilk to the dry ingredients and mix in with your hands. It should be soft – not too wet and sticky.

Place the mixture into a 1kg greased tin and give the tin a bang on the bottom so the mixture sinks evenly. Wet your hands to stop the mixture sticking to them and lightly press it down so it is evenly spread in the tin.

Bake for 45 minutes. Then remove the bread from the tin, return to the oven and cook for another 15 minutes. If in doubt, tap the bottom of the bread. When you hear a hollow sound, it's cooked. Cool on a wire rack.

# ROCKET, SUN-DRIED TOMATO & MOZZARELLA LOAF

MAKES 1 LOAF

## INGREDIENTS

250g strong flour

4g salt

18g yeast

150ml warm water

100g grated mozzarella

100g sun-dried tomatoes, chopped

Pinch of Cajun spice

1 bunch of fresh rocket, chopped

1 egg

1 tsp milk

## METHOD

In a bowl, mix the flour and the salt. Whisk the yeast into the warm water, then add to the dry mixture. You need to knead the dough for 3 minutes – if you have a stand mixer with a dough hook, that's brilliant; if you don't, you'll have to use your hands.

Add the mozzarella, sun-dried tomatoes, Cajun spice and rocket, and mix for 2 more minutes to bind the ingredients together.

Once the bread is kneaded, turn it onto your counter and form it into a smooth ball with your hands. If it's a bit wet, add a little more flour. Put the dough into a bowl and cover with cling film. Let it rise in the warmest place in your kitchen until it doubles in size. I usually leave mine for an hour.

Turn the risen dough out onto a lightly floured counter. Using your hands, press it out into a rectangle shape about 25 mm in thickness, then roll the dough tightly along its length.

Transfer the dough to a greased 1kg tin and push the dough into the edges of the tin. Let it rise again for roughly 20 minutes. While it's proving, preheat the oven to 180°C.

Beat the egg and milk together and brush the dough with this egg wash. Bake for 40–45 minutes until golden brown and the loaf sounds hollow when tapped underneath.

# WALNUT & BANANA BREAD

SERVES 8

## INGREDIENTS

225g plain flour

1 tsp salt

1 tsp baking powder

1 tsp ground cinnamon

100g caster sugar

1 egg, beaten

75ml sunflower oil

2 drops vanilla essence

40g carrot, grated

70g roasted walnuts, crushed

4 ripe bananas, mashed

ICING

150g soft butter

150g icing sugar

150g cream cheese

TOPPINGS

1 banana

Grated walnuts

## METHOD

Preheat the oven to 180°C.

Sift the flour, salt, baking powder and cinnamon into a bowl and stir in the sugar.

In a separate bowl, mix the egg, sunflower oil, vanilla essence and grated carrot together, then mix the wet and dry ingredients together.

Fold in the roasted walnuts and add the banana, combining well. Pour your mixture into a greased 1kg tin and bake for 1 hour. Use a skewer to check if the bread is cooked. Insert this into the middle of the bread – if it comes out clean, then the loaf is cooked. If not, cook for a further 5 minutes and check again.

Once the loaf is cooked, leave it to cool in the tin for 10 minutes.

For the icing, mix the butter, icing sugar and cream cheese together, then pour over the bread, covering it completely. Slice the banana on top and, finally, sprinkle with the grated walnut.

❋TIP:
Roast the walnuts in the oven for 5–7 minutes to get the best flavour from them.

# TEA CAKE WITH BRANDY ICING

**SERVES 6—8**

## INGREDIENTS

150g brown sugar
100ml tea
1 tsp whiskey
150g sultanas
150g mixed fruit
3 eggs, beaten
150g plain flour
1 tsp baking powder
1 tsp mixed spice
1 tsp maple syrup
Zest of 1 orange

BRANDY ICING
150g soft butter
100g icing sugar
150g cream cheese
2 tsp brandy

## METHOD

Dissolve the sugar in the tea, then mix in the whiskey and fruit. Soak the fruit overnight.

Preheat the oven to 170°C and line a cake tin (approximately 1kg) with greaseproof paper.

Mix the eggs, flour, baking powder and mixed spice into the fruit mixture, then pour into the tin. Bake for 50 minutes and test with a skewer. If it comes out clean, it's cooked. If not, cook for another 5 minutes and test again.

Once the cake is cooked, remove it from the tin and brush with maple syrup while it's still hot.

For the brandy icing, mix all the ingredients together. When the tea cake is cool, layer the icing on top of the cake and then grate some orange zest on top to finish.

# ROSEMARY, TOMATO & GREEN OLIVE FOCACCIA

SERVES 8

## INGREDIENTS

40g yeast

500g strong flour

1 tsp salt

2 tsp olive oil, plus extra for drizzling

### TOPPING

1 tsp roughly chopped rosemary

100g tomatoes (no seeds), chopped

100g green olives, pitted

1 tsp sea salt

1 tsp semolina

100g white cheddar, grated

## METHOD

Whisk the yeast in 250ml of warm water until it dissolves.

Put your flour, salt and olive oil into the bowl of a stand mixer, followed by the yeast mixture. Using a dough hook, slowly mix for about 5 minutes. Then put into a bowl and cover with cling film. Allow the dough to prove for 30 minutes – it should double in size.

When the dough has risen, remove from the bowl and knead once more by hand. Then place the dough on a greased baking tray 30 x 25 cm, spreading it into all four corners. Poke it all over with your fingers to make mini wells. Cover with a damp cloth and leave to rise again for 15–20 minutes.

While the dough is proving, preheat the oven to 180°C.

Drizzle olive oil all over the dough, then top with the rosemary, tomatoes, green olives and sea salt, and sprinkle the semolina on top. Bake in the oven for 20 minutes. Then sprinkle over the grated cheese and allow to cook for a further 5 minutes.

♨VARIATION:
Another one of my favourite focaccia toppings is red chilli, rocket and red onion.

# ROCO'S QUICHE

Quiche is so easy to make once you get the base right. I prefer to use a fluted 24 cm tin with a removable base. It is important to note that you must always cook your meat before adding it to the egg mixture.

SERVES 8

## INGREDIENTS

350g plain flour

175g butter

2 eggs

1 tsp milk

FILLING

½ red onion, diced

Olive oil

4 eggs, plus 1 extra yolk

350ml cream

150g ham, diced

100g white cheddar cheese, grated

1 tsp chopped chives

FILLING VARIATIONS:

Smoked chicken, feta and baby spinach (fry the chicken and spinach first)

Pancetta, mushroom and Applewood cheddar (fry the pancetta and mushroom first)

Red peppers, sweetcorn, broad bean and feta cheese (fry the peppers first)

Smoked salmon, crab and Gruyère cheese

Crispy bacon, red cheddar, spring onion and black pudding (fry the bacon and pudding first)

## METHOD

First make the pastry. Combine the flour and butter until it resembles breadcrumbs, then add 1 egg, followed by 2 teaspoons of cold water. Mix lightly to bring the dough together to create a smooth solid ball. Wrap in cling film and set in the fridge for 20 minutes.

Preheat the oven to 190°C.

Grease your tin so the pastry does not stick. Roll out the pastry so that it is large enough to cover the base and sides of a 24 cm fluted quiche tin. Line the tin with the pastry, making sure the sides are tucked in well, then line the pastry with parchment paper and dried beans, and blind bake for 20 minutes. Beat together 1 egg and the milk. Remove the paper and beans, egg wash the base and cook for a further 4–6 minutes, until the pastry is golden. Hopefully, when cooked there will be no cracks!

Turn down the oven to 165°C.

Now for the filling. Sauté the diced onion in a pan with a drop of oil until cooked, then remove from the pan and allow to cool.

Mix the 4 eggs and extra yolk in a bowl with the cream. Add the ham, cheese and the cooled cooked onion to the egg mix. Once mixed, add the chopped chives.

Pour the filling into the base and bake in the oven for 40–45 minutes. When cooked, the middle of the quiche will be firm to touch. Serve with a nice garden-leaf salad.

# OLIVE OIL & LEMON VERBENA CAKE

SERVES 8–10

## INGREDIENTS

4 eggs

200g caster sugar

Juice and zest of 1 lemon

1 tsp chopped lemon verbena

100ml olive oil

100g butter, melted

200g ground almonds

50g polenta

50g plain flour

1 tsp baking powder

Icing sugar, to dust

Lemon zest, to serve

### BLUEBERRY JAM

300g blueberries (fresh or frozen)

Juice of ½ lemon

2 tsp blueberry juice

50g caster sugar

8g pectin

## METHOD

Preheat the oven to 180°C. Grease and line the base of a 23 cm loose-bottomed cake tin.

Put the eggs, caster sugar, lemon zest and lemon verbena in a mixing bowl, and whisk until thick and creamy. The mixture should be at the ribbon stage – when the whisk is lifted from the mixture it should leave ribbons on the surface.

Slowly whisk in the lemon juice, olive oil and melted butter until combined.

In a separate bowl, mix together the ground almonds, polenta, flour and baking powder. Gently fold the wet and dry mixtures together, then pour into the greased baking tin and bake for 35 minutes. To check if it's cooked, insert a small knife into the centre. It should come out a little damp but not coated in cake mix. If ready, remove the tin from the oven and allow to cool.

To make the jam, put the blueberries in a small saucepan with the lemon and blueberry juices and the caster sugar. Bring to the boil. Sprinkle over the pectin and stir to dissolve. Simmer for a further 5 minutes. Remove from the heat and leave to cool slightly.

Place the cake onto a round plate and dust with icing sugar and lemon zest. Serve the jam on the side.

# GLUTEN-FREE CHOCOLATE & ORANGE CAKE

SERVES 8

## INGREDIENTS

1 vanilla pod

180g soft butter

180g brown sugar

6 eggs, separated

180g dark chocolate (70%)

Zest of 2 oranges, finely grated

1 tsp orange essence

180g ground almonds

2 tsp cocoa powder for dusting

## METHOD

Heat the oven to 180°C. Grease a 23 cm spring-form cake tin well. It's very important that you grease the tin properly or the cake will stick.

Split the vanilla pod lengthways and scrape out the seeds. Beat together the butter, sugar and vanilla seeds, and whisk until light and creamy. Add the egg yolks, making sure they are mixed well.

Melt the chocolate in a bowl set over a pot of simmering water. When melted, add the orange zest and essence and the ground almonds, and mix well.

Combine the chocolate mixture with the creamed butter and sugar. In a separate bowl, whisk the egg whites until they form soft peaks. Add a third of the egg white to the chocolate mixture and combine gently. Then fold in the remaining egg white.

Gently transfer to your greased cake tin and bake for 45 minutes. The cake should be firm. Stick a small knife in the centre, and if it comes out clean then the cake is cooked. Usually I would dust this with some cocoa powder before serving, or make an orange icing.

# THE BURKES' CHRISTMAS CAKE

You can make this up to six weeks before Christmas. Wrap in a double layer of parchment paper
and then tinfoil, and store in an airtight container in a dry cool place.

MAKES 1 LARGE CAKE

## INGREDIENTS

685g mixed dried fruit

110g nibbed almonds

110g candied mixed peel, chopped

110g glacé cherries, halved

300g plain flour

1 tsp ground cinnamon

1 tsp ground nutmeg

Juice and zest of 2 oranges

Juice and zest of 1 lemon

220g salted butter

220g brown sugar

1 tsp vanilla essence

1 tsp black treacle

4 eggs, beaten

½ tsp bread soda

12 tsp whole milk

3 tsp Jameson whiskey

MARZIPAN

400g icing sugar

500g ground almonds

2 eggs, beaten

4 tsp lemon juice

2 tsp apricot jam

Icing sugar, to dust

## METHOD

Preheat the oven to 140°C and line a 20 cm cake tin with a double layer of parchment paper, leaving a couple of centimetres sticking up from the top.

With your hands, mix the dried fruit, almonds, peel and cherries in a bowl. Then add the flour, cinnamon, nutmeg and lemon and orange zest and juice. Combine well.

Cream the butter with the sugar, then add the vanilla essence and treacle. While mixing these together, add the eggs, and mix until well combined. Then add your wet mixture to the dried fruit mixture.

Dissolve the bread soda in the milk and add to the mixture. Make sure you give this a good stir. Add your Jameson and stir again. Pour your mixture into the lined baking tin and bake for 3 hours. Check if it's cooked using a wooden skewer. If the skewer comes out dry, it's ready. It might need another 20–30 minutes. Once cooked, leave to cool in its tin.

To make the marzipan, sift the sugar into a bowl and mix with the ground almonds. Add the beaten eggs and the lemon juice and mix until fully combined into a smooth dough. Wrap in cling film and to leave rest in the fridge.

When you are ready to ice the cake, boil the apricot jam with 1 teaspoon of water. Leave to cool slightly and when still warm brush a thin layer of jam all over the cake.

ICING

4 egg whites

6 tsp lemon juice

1kg icing sugar

On a surface dusted with icing sugar, roll the marzipan to 5 mm in thickness. Using your rolling pin, lift the marzipan and cover the cake, pushing it onto the sides. Trim off any excess marzipan and allow to dry for 3 hours.

For the icing, whisk the egg whites until they are white and foamy but not stiff. Add the lemon juice, then add the sugar bit by bit. Continue to beat the mixture until it is pure white. Cover the bowl and leave for 1 hour before using.

Place your icing on the cake. Start at the top, and with a warm, dry palette knife, spread your icing all over the top and sides of the cake, covering every inch and leaving it smooth. Now it's up to yourself to decorate your cake with whatever you like – be adventurous. Myself and Maisie had a bit of fun finishing ours with Christmas decorations.

❉TIP:
To spread your icing evenly, dip a palette knife into warm water, then dry before using.

STARTERS

# CROCK OF GLENBEIGH MUSSELS

SERVES 4 (OR 2 AS A MAIN COURSE)

## INGREDIENTS

2kg fresh mussels

1 tsp vegetable oil

1 carrot, finely chopped

1 small white onion, finely chopped

2 sticks of celery, finely chopped

6 cloves of garlic, finely chopped

2 sticks of lemon grass

50g ginger, peeled

2 red chillies, sliced

300ml white wine

500ml coconut milk

Large handful of fresh coriander, chopped

Coriander leaves, spring onion and red chilli, to garnish

## METHOD

First clean the mussels carefully, discard any broken shells or any opened ones. Wash under cold water to remove any grit or dirt.

Heat a large saucepan over a medium heat, then add your vegetable oil, followed by all your finely chopped vegetables, the lemon grass, ginger and chillies. Sauté for at least 4 minutes to release all the flavours without colouring.

Add the wine and mussels and cook for 10 minutes with the lid on. Give the mussels a good shake every 2 minutes so they cook evenly.

When cooked, drain the liquid into another saucepan and bring to the boil. Once the mussel stock is bubbling, add your coconut milk. When that comes to the boil, reduce the heat and leave to simmer for a further 5 minutes to reduce. Then add the chopped coriander.

To serve, divide the mussels into four bowls and pour the sauce over the mussels. Garnish with some fresh coriander leaves and some sliced spring onion and red chilli. Serve with crusty garlic bread to soak up the coconut cream.

# CRISPY TEMPURA OF VEGETABLES

SERVES 4–6

## INGREDIENTS

TEMPURA BATTER

130g cornflour

1 egg, beaten

200ml sparkling water

Pinch of salt

1 tsp black sesame seeds

Pinch of saffron strands

VEGETABLES

1 courgette, halved lengthways and cut into wedges

1 aubergine, cut into wedges

1 bunch of asparagus tips

1 small head of cauliflower, quartered and cut into wedges

1 yellow pepper, cored and cut into six pieces, lengthways

1 red pepper, cored and cut into six pieces, lengthways

BLUE CHEESE DRESSING

50g blue cheese

40g sour cream

40g mayonnaise

Juice and zest of 1 lime

1 tsp chopped chives

2 tsp cream

## METHOD

First make your batter. Put the cornflour in a bowl, followed by the egg. Slowly add the water, whisking constantly. You should have no lumps and the batter should be nice and smooth, then add the salt and sesame seeds.

Add 1 teaspoon of boiling water to the saffron strands. This will react with the saffron, turning the colour to a bright yellow. Add this to the batter and mix, then leave in the fridge until ready for use.

Preheat a deep-fat fryer to 180°C. If you don't have a fryer, fill a pot with enough oil to fully cover the vegetables as they fry and heat to 180°C – use a thermometer to check. Dip the vegetables in the batter, shaking off any excess, and gently place them into the hot oil. Keep turning the vegetables until nice and crispy. Once they are ready, take out and put on kitchen paper to remove any excess oil.

For the blue cheese dressing, blend all the ingredients together. Serve in a ramekin on the side.

✳TIP:
You could also use this tempura recipe for fish: squid, prawns and sole are all beautiful. We have that on our menu plenty.

♨VARIATION:
Change your sauce to chilli jam or wasabi if you want it spicier. For the batter, you could add some fennel seeds instead of black sesame seeds.

# CHILLI BEEF & BABY GEM WRAPS, BLUE CHEESE & TOASTED CASHEW NUTS

This is a nice light dish. You could also try lamb instead of beef mince. Serve with raita (see p. 66).

SERVES 4

## INGREDIENTS

1 tsp olive oil

400g steak mince

Salt and black pepper

1 tsp sesame oil

1 red or green chilli, chopped

4 cloves of garlic, chopped

1 tsp fish sauce

Juice and zest of 1 lime

8 leaves of baby gem lettuce

30g blue cheese

A handful of cashew nuts, toasted

Spring onion and red chilli, to garnish

### DRESSING

1 tsp soy sauce

Juice and zest of 1 lime

1 tsp sesame oil

1 tsp olive oil

1 tsp honey

1 tsp chopped chives

1 tsp chopped coriander

## METHOD

Heat a large frying pan over a medium heat, then add the olive oil and fry the mince, seasoned with salt and pepper, for 5–8 minutes. Once the mince is crisp and broken down to a fine consistency, drain it in a sieve.

Add your sesame oil to the same pan and fry the chilli and garlic until cooked. Then return the mince to the pan and add the fish sauce and lime juice and zest. Taste for seasoning. It should have a light chilli kick, but not overpower the meat.

Make your dressing by combining all of the ingredients in a bowl.

To assemble, place two leaves of baby gem on each plate. Fill with the mince mixture, crumble a little blue cheese on the top of each, and sprinkle with your toasted cashew nuts. Garnish with really thinly sliced spring onion and red chilli. Serve with your dressing on the side.

# DUCK PASTILLA ROLL WITH ROASTED PLUMS & GUACAMOLE

SERVES 4

## INGREDIENTS

1 tsp olive oil

1 large red pepper, finely sliced

1 large green pepper, finely sliced

2 cloves of garlic, chopped

1 large red onion, finely sliced

3 tsp hoisin sauce

1 tsp chilli sauce

600g cooked duck, shredded

1 tsp chopped coriander

8 sheets brick or spring-roll pastry (*feuille de brick* is the best as it's light and crispy, but spring roll is fine)

1 egg, beaten

Vegetable oil

### PLUM JAM

4 plums

4 tsp white sugar

Pinch of ground cinnamon

Pinch of ground star anise

### GUACAMOLE

3 avocados, peeled and chopped

1 plum tomato, deseeded and chopped

½ red chilli, deseeded and chopped

1 tsp chopped coriander

1 spring onion, chopped

Juice of 1 lemon

## METHOD

Heat the oil in a pan over a medium heat, then fry off your peppers, garlic and red onion until soft and cooked. Once cooked, add the hoisin and chilli sauces. Cook for a further 3 minutes, then remove from the heat and allow to cool.

Mix the shredded duck with the fresh coriander, then add to the cooled vegetables and combine.

For the plum jam, cut the plums in half, removing the stone. Put in a non-stick pan with the sugar and ground cinnamon and star anise and cook slowly for 15 minutes. If the plums are hard, add 1 teaspoon of water.

For the guacamole, mix all the ingredients together and cover.

To assemble, lay one sheet of pastry on a work surface and brush with a little egg. Place another sheet of pastry on top and gently press down. Place a quarter of your duck mixture at one end of the pastry, leaving the edges of the pastry exposed, and brush with a little egg around the sides. Fold in the end, followed by the sides, and roll up the pastry like a cigar.

Heat your pan over a medium heat and add enough vegetable oil for deep-fat frying. Then add the pastry roll and cook until golden brown. This should take 5–7 minutes. If you have a deep-fat fryer, cook at 180°C for 5 minutes until golden brown.

To serve, cut the ends off the spring-roll pastry using a serrated knife. This will help it to stand on the plate. Then cut it in the middle at an angle. Serve with some guacamole and plums.

### ⚶ VARIATION:
Instead of duck, you can use chicken, fish (salmon is good), or even shellfish, such as crab.

# CHICKEN-LIVER PARFAIT WITH FIG & APPLE CHUTNEY

SERVES 8—10

## INGREDIENTS

600g fresh chicken livers

1 tsp ground pink salt (normal salt is fine)

100ml red wine

100ml port

1 shallot, chopped

3 cloves of garlic

2 sprigs of thyme

2 sprigs of rosemary

3 eggs, beaten

600g salted butter, melted

### CHUTNEY

150g apples, peeled and diced

150g figs, diced

100g white onion, diced

Juice and zest of 2 oranges

2 star anise

350g caster sugar

1 cinnamon stick

50g golden raisins

1 litre apple juice

1 tsp cayenne pepper

200ml white-wine vinegar

## METHOD

Preheat the oven to 160°C.

Place the chicken livers in a bowl and season with the salt.

Put the red wine, port, shallot, garlic and fresh herbs in a pot over a high heat. Reduce by half. This should take 5 minutes.

Pour the hot wine sauce over the livers and mix with a spoon. Transfer the mixture to a food processor and blend. Then add the eggs and melted butter and blend once again until nice and smooth. Finally, pass the mixture through a fine sieve into a large jug.

Line a metal 1 litre loaf tin with cling film and pour in the chicken and wine mixture. It should come two-thirds of the way up the sides. Cover the top with tinfoil and place in a roasting tin half filled with water. Cook in the oven for 1¼ hours until set but still with a slight wobble in the middle. When the parfait is cooked, remove the tin from the bain-marie, take off the foil and leave to cool overnight.

For the chutney, place all the ingredients into a pot and slowly cook on a low heat for 1½ hours, stirring frequently, until the liquid has reduced by two-thirds. Before serving, remove the cinnamon stick and star anise.

When ready to serve, turn the parfait onto a board and peel away the cling film. I usually soften butter and spread it evenly all over the parfait with a palette knife, which gives a touch of elegance. Heat a large knife in boiling water, then dry it and slice the parfait. Put slices on a plate and sprinkle some sea salt on top. Place some chutney on the side and a slice of toasted sourdough.

# BUFFALO MOZZARELLA, CHARGRILLED VEGETABLES & ROCKET PESTO BRUSCHETTA

SERVES 4

## INGREDIENTS

1 red pepper, halved and deseeded

1 yellow pepper, halved and deseeded

Olive oil

1 courgette, sliced

1 aubergine, sliced

4 basil leaves, chopped

Salt and black pepper, to season

4 slices of crusty bread (sourdough)

3 cloves of garlic, peeled

2 buffalo mozzarella, sliced thinly

40g baby rocket leaves, to serve

Hummus, to serve

### ROCKET PESTO

1 bunch of rocket

1 bunch of basil

2 cloves of garlic

1 tsp grated Parmesan

200ml olive oil

Squeeze of lemon juice

## METHOD

Rub the red and yellow peppers with olive oil. Put on a hot griddle or frying pan and chargrill to a slightly black colour, then put into a bowl and cover with cling film straight away. (If you have it, a ridged griddle pan is perfect, but if not a normal pan will do just fine.) When they are cool enough to handle, remove the skin.

Rub the sliced courgette and aubergine with olive oil and chargrill on both sides, creating a lovely criss-cross effect if you are using a griddle.

Mix all the vegetables together in a bowl with the chopped basil and a drop of olive oil. Season with salt and pepper.

Preheat the oven to 180°C. Cut four slices of sourdough, rub them with the garlic and drizzle with a little olive oil. Chargrill on both sides.

For the rocket pesto, blitz all the ingredients together in a blender until you form a smooth paste.

To assemble the dish, place some of the vegetables on each slice of toast and add two thin slices of mozzarella. Drizzle some rocket pesto on top, then bake in the oven for 10–12 minutes until nice and crispy. Serve with rocket leaves and hummus on the side.

### ⚒VARIATIONS:
You can try loads of different toppings, such as pastrami, Parma ham, smoked chicken or goats' cheese. Be adventurous and come up with your own.

# CARRIGTWOHILL
# BAKED POTATOES

SERVES 4

## INGREDIENTS

4 large baking potatoes

6 rashers

200g crème fraîche

2 spring onions, finely sliced

Juice and zest of 1 lime

½ red chilli, freshly chopped

Salt and pepper

60g butter

A handful of fresh chives, chopped

150g grated cheddar

## METHOD

Preheat the oven to 180°C. Wash the potatoes and wrap in tinfoil. Place them on a baking tray and bake them in the oven for roughly 1 hour until cooked. The potato will be slightly soft to touch.

Cook the bacon under the grill until nice and crispy. Cool and chop roughly.

Mix the crème fraîche, spring onions, lime juice and zest and chilli together. Add salt and pepper to taste.

When the baked potatoes are cooked, take them out and allow them to cool slightly. (Leave the oven on.) Cut them lengthways and scoop out the flesh. In a bowl, mash the potato with the butter, then add the rashers and chives, half the grated cheese and salt and pepper to taste.

Arrange the potato skins on a baking tray, divide the filling between them and sprinkle the rest of the cheese on top. Return to the oven and bake for 15–20 minutes. Serve with a salad and place the crème fraîche on top, or leave on the side if you prefer.

VARIATIONS:
If you want a vegetarian option, just use red pepper and sweetcorn instead of bacon. Mess around, come up with your own baked potato!

# POSH SAUSAGE ROLL WITH HOME-MADE KETCHUP

SERVES 6—8

## INGREDIENTS

300g sausage meat

100g black pudding, out of its casing

1 small onion, diced

50g breadcrumbs

1 tsp Dijon mustard

4 tsp cream

Salt and black pepper

2 sheets of pre-rolled puff pastry (usually 320g each)

Flour for dusting

1 egg, beaten

1 tsp mixed sesame seeds

### KETCHUP

1 tsp olive oil

1 carrot, finely diced

1 stick of celery, finely diced

1 medium onion, finely diced

4 cloves of garlic, chopped

5g fresh ginger, chopped

3 tsp tomato paste

1 tsp rice vinegar

800g chopped tomatoes

800g plum tomatoes, chopped

5g fresh oregano, chopped

## METHOD

Preheat the oven to 180°C.

Mix together the sausage meat, black pudding, onion, breadcrumbs, mustard and cream, and season with salt and pepper to taste. Fry a little of the mixture in a pan to check the seasoning. Fill a large piping bag (no nozzle) with the mix; if you don't have a piping bag, you can use a spoon.

Lay out the puff pastry sheets on a lightly floured counter. Then squeeze a line of sausage mix along the long edge of the pastry – about 10 cm in from the edge. Roll up the pastry, brushing the far edge with egg mix to help seal it closed. Cut each sheet into two or three pieces, whichever you prefer. With a sharp knife, trim the ends off the sausage rolls. Brush with more egg mix and sprinkle with the mixed seeds.

Put your sausage rolls on a baking tray and bake in the oven for 20 minutes or until golden brown.

To make the ketchup, heat a pan with the olive oil over a medium heat, then add the carrot, celery, onion, garlic and fresh ginger. Once soft and cooked, add the tomato paste and vinegar. Cook for 1 minute, then add the chopped and plum tomatoes. Cook slowly for 30–45 minutes until thick.

Add the fresh herbs to the tomatoes and blitz, then pass through a strainer. Put back on the heat with the red-wine vinegar and brown sugar, and bring to the boil.

5g fresh basil, chopped

150ml red-wine vinegar

50g brown sugar

Once boiled, turn down the heat and leave to reduce by half. This should take 10–12 minutes. Check the seasoning. It should taste like a good balance of sweet and sour, but if it's a bit bitter add some more sugar. This will sweeten the sauce.

Once the ketchup is ready, allow to cool, then serve a dollop with your sausage rolls.

# PRAWNS PIL-PIL WITH RAITA & BLACK OLIVE TOASTED LOAF

If you are not a fan of black olives, just do normal garlic bread.

SERVES 4–6

## INGREDIENTS

200ml extra virgin olive oil

800g large prawns, peeled and deveined

1 red chilli, chopped

1 green chilli, chopped

6 cloves of garlic, finely sliced

5g fresh ginger, grated

100g tomatoes, chopped

1 tsp chopped chives

1 tsp chopped coriander

1 spring onion, finely sliced

Juice of 1 lemon

Salt, to season (optional)

4–6 slices of crusty bread

### BLACK OLIVE TAPENADE

100g pitted black olives

2 cloves of garlic

50ml olive oil

A handful of fresh parsley

### RAITA

½ cucumber, grated

150ml yoghurt

2 tsp chopped mint

Zest of 1 lime

## METHOD

Preheat the oven to 180°C.

Heat the olive oil in a non-stick pan on the hob. Add the prawns and sauté for 3 minutes. Then add the red and green chillies, garlic and ginger, and continue to sauté for 2 more minutes, until the prawns are cooked.

Add your chopped tomatoes, fresh chives, coriander, spring onion and lemon juice, and toss together with the prawns. Check for seasoning. It might need some salt or a bit more lemon juice, depending on your own taste.

To make the tapenade, place all the ingredients into a blender and blitz until nice and smooth.

To make the raita, just mix all the ingredients together.

Cut a nice slice of crusty bread for each person, and spread some tapenade thinly onto the bread. Bake for 4–6 minutes until nice and crispy. Serve the prawns in a bowl with your crispy black olive bread on the side, and serve the raita in a side dish.

# 'SATURDAY NIGHT NACHOS'

This is fun, easy and tasty with a bottle of beer or glass of wine.

SERVES 4

## INGREDIENTS

400g nachos

100g refried beans

50g jalapeño peppers, sliced

50g whole pitted black olives

100g smoked cheddar

100g sour cream

100g guacamole (see p. 53)

50g spicy salsa

A handful of chives, finely chopped

## METHOD

Preheat the oven to 180°C.

Put half of your nachos in an ovenproof bowl and put half of your beans, jalapeños, black olives and cheddar on top. Put into the oven for 4 minutes. Repeat the process with the rest of the ingredients and cook for another 4 minutes.

Once the nachos are ready, don't be shy with the sour cream – lash it on! Then add the guacamole and salsa, and sprinkle some fresh chives on top to show off.

❋TIP:
There are loads of variations you could do with mincemeat and chicken. Nachos are fun.

# TED'S SMOKED HADDOCK FISHCAKES WITH SWEETCORN PURÉE, RED PEPPER AIOLI AND CRISPY CAPERS

I get my locally smoked haddock from Ted and Brendan at Gulf Stream Seafoods in Kenmare.

SERVES 4

## INGREDIENTS

500g rooster potatoes, peeled and roughly chopped

700g smoked haddock, diced

½ lime

1 sprig of fresh parsley

1 tsp chopped chives

½ red chilli, deseeded and chopped

1 spring onion, finely chopped

Juice and zest of 1 lemon

Salt, to season

75g plain flour

2 eggs, beaten

100g fresh breadcrumbs

2 tsp capers

SWEETCORN PURÉE

200g sweetcorn

300ml vegetable stock

30g butter

RED PEPPER AIOLI

2 red peppers, roasted

3 cloves of garlic

1 tsp fresh coriander

100g mayonnaise

## METHOD

Put the potatoes into a pot and cover with salted water. Bring to the boil and leave to simmer until they are cooked (roughly 20 minutes). Once ready, mash well – don't leave any lumps!

Put the diced haddock into a pot and cover with water. Add half a lime and a sprig of fresh parsley. Bring to the boil and leave to simmer for 4 minutes. Strain, remove the lime and parsley, and place the haddock in a bowl.

Add the potato mash to the fish with the chives, chilli, spring onion and lemon juice and zest, and mix. Add salt to taste for seasoning. Mould the fish cakes into eight balls – each roughly the size of a golf ball – and put them in the fridge to rest and chill for at least 1 hour. If you prefer not to deep fry, make four patties instead.

To make the purée, put the sweetcorn in a pot and cover it with the vegetable stock. Once the stock comes to the boil, leave to simmer for 20 minutes. When it is cooked it should be nice and soft. Strain, then blitz in a blender. Add the butter and blitz again. Pass through a fine sieve until it's a purée – nice and smooth.

For the aioli, put the peppers, garlic and coriander in a blender and blitz to a fine purée. Add the mayonnaise and blitz for ten more seconds.

Roll the fishcakes in the flour, completely coating them, then dip in the beaten egg and finally roll in the breadcrumbs.

If you don't have a deep-fat fryer, preheat the oven to 180°C. For the fryer, pour 1 litre of vegetable oil into a pot and bring to the same temperature. Check with a thermometer to make sure the temperature is correct. Cook the fishcakes in the fryer for roughly 5 minutes. They should be nice and golden brown and crispy on the outside. If you are pan-frying, heat a non-stick pan, add 1 teaspoon of olive oil and fry on either side for 2 minutes each. Finish in the oven for 8 minutes.

Deep-fry the capers in a pot until crispy, roughly 1 minute.

To plate up, put a spoonful of the sweetcorn purée on the plate and then arrange two fishcakes on top, with dots of the red pepper aioli to garnish. Sprinkle deep-fried capers on top and add some pea shoots if you have them.

# TIMOLEAGUE STICKY PORK RIBS

SERVES 4

## INGREDIENTS

2kg (full rack) pork ribs

Sea salt and pepper

2 tsp five spice

2 tsp chilli flakes

1 tsp olive oil

1 litre beef stock

2 whole star anise

1 tsp toasted sesame seeds

### HONEY & PINEAPPLE GLAZE

50g salted butter, diced

1 fresh pineapple, diced

100ml soy sauce

100ml hoisin sauce

100ml honey

100ml ketchup

5 tsp rice vinegar

1 red chilli, chopped

20g fresh ginger, chopped

## METHOD

Preheat the oven to 180°C.

Season the pork ribs with salt and pepper, and then the five spice and chilli flakes.

Heat a roasting pan on the hob to a high heat. Add the oil and brown the ribs all over. Once nicely coloured, add the beef stock and star anise, cover with a lid or tinfoil and cook for 2½ hours in the oven until the meat is tender.

To prepare the glaze, melt the butter, then add the pineapple and cook over a medium heat for 5 minutes until slightly caramelised. Add the soy sauce, hoisin sauce, honey, ketchup, rice vinegar, chilli and ginger, and slowly cook for 30 minutes.

Allow to cool a bit, then pour the glaze into a blender and blitz until a smooth purée.

When they are cooked, baste the ribs with the pineapple glaze. Return to the oven and cook for another 10 minutes. Sprinkle with toasted sesame seeds and serve.

# CASTLETOWNBERE SCALLOPS, PANCETTA & GARDEN PEAS WITH PEA CREAM

This is the show-stopper if you want to impress at a dinner party – you will be talked about for weeks. It's a pretty, tasty and class-act starter.

SERVES 4

## INGREDIENTS

150g pancetta, diced

1 clove of garlic, chopped

½ shallot, diced

Olive oil

150g peas (if frozen, thaw before using)

1 tsp chopped fresh mint

8 large scallops

Sea salt

20g hard butter

½ lemon

### PEA CREAM SAUCE

2 cloves of garlic

½ shallot, diced

1 tsp olive oil

400g fresh peas

400ml vegetable stock

1 tsp cream

Sea salt

## METHOD

First get your sauce made. In a pot on a low heat, sauté the garlic and shallot in the olive oil until soft, but don't allow them to colour.

Add your peas and cook for 5 more minutes. Then add the hot vegetable stock to the peas and cook for a further 2 minutes. Blitz and pass through a fine strainer so it's nice and smooth. Add the cream and then season with salt to taste to make sure it isn't bland. Set aside and keep warm until needed.

In a pan, fry the pancetta, garlic and shallot with a dash of olive oil until crispy. Add the peas and cook for a further 3 minutes. Add the fresh mint at the last second. Turn off the heat and set aside.

Season the scallops with sea salt. Then heat a non-stick pan until nice and hot. Add some olive oil, then the scallops. Fry on one side for 2 minutes, then add the butter and turn the scallops over. Cook on the other side for 2 more minutes, basting the scallops with a spoon until they are caramelised and cooked. Place on a plate and squeeze a little lemon juice on top.

To plate up, here comes the theatre. Put the pea cream into a sauce jug. Place the peas and pancetta in the middle of your bowl with the scallops on top. If you can get edible flowers to surround the scallops, that will be some fancy stuff. Place your bowl in front of your guest and pour the sauce around the scallops. Well done, chef. Take a bow!

# ROCO'S SUPERFOOD SALAD

You won't believe the energy this salad will bring you –
running a marathon would be easy after eating this, and it's great for me as a parent running after my kids.

SERVES 4

## INGREDIENTS

200g cooked green beans

200g cooked beetroot

2 avocados

100g cherry tomatoes

4 sticks of celery

½ cucumber, sliced

100g whole walnuts

200g cooked pinto beans

2 tsp pumpkin seeds

20g baby leaves

100g baby spinach leaves

200g feta cheese, diced

### ROCO'S HOUSE DRESSING

2 tsp Dijon mustard

2 tsp local honey

50ml white-wine vinegar

200ml olive oil

1 tsp chopped chives

1 tsp chopped parsley

Salt and pepper

## METHOD

Nice and simple. Get a big bowl. Roughly chop your green beans, beetroot, avocados, tomatoes, celery and cucumber, and add them all to the bowl.

Add your walnuts, pinto beans (if using canned, make sure to strain them and give a good wash under the cold tap), pumpkin seeds, washed baby leaves and spinach, and then toss.

For our house dressing, first whisk the mustard, honey and vinegar in a bowl, then slowly add the oil. The mixture will get thicker. At the end, add the fresh herbs and season with salt and pepper. Once made, add to the tossed salad.

Divide into four bowls and crumble equal portions of feta on top.

### ♨ VARIATIONS:
You can make different salads by adding chicken, beef, salmon, crab or prawn.

# WEST CORK BBQ BEEF SALAD WITH FRANCISCAN WELL BEER DRESSING

When buying the beef, go to a butcher's and ask for thin beef strips using rump –
it's a lot cheaper than sirloin and fillet steak, but it tastes just as good.

SERVES 4

## INGREDIENTS

600g beef strips

20g BBQ powder or seasoning

Olive oil

400g baby potatoes

1 tsp chopped garlic

1 tsp chopped parsley

200g stem broccoli

400g rocket

100g cherry tomatoes, halved

100g gherkins, sliced

1 large carrot, grated

100g roasted cashew nuts

150g blue cheese or Parmesan

### BEER DRESSING

3 tsp olive oil

1 shallot, finely diced

1 tsp pulled fresh thyme

330ml Franciscan Well 'Friar Weisse' beer

1 tsp honey

1 tsp white-wine vinegar

1 tsp Dijon mustard

## METHOD

Get your beef mixed with the BBQ powder and 1 teaspoon of olive oil and put in the fridge. The longer it marinates the better. Go for 3 hours minimum, but overnight is better.

Cook your baby potatoes in salted water until soft, which will take roughly 20 minutes. When cool, slice in half.

Preheat the oven to 170°C. Heat a non-stick pan and add 2 teaspoons of olive oil and the chopped garlic. Cook the garlic for 1 minute and then add the potatoes. Once you get a colour on the potatoes, add the parsley. Transfer to an ovenproof dish or small flat tray and cook in the oven for another 10 minutes.

Put the stem broccoli in a pot of boiling salted water and cook for 1 minute. That's all it takes. Refresh in ice-cold water.

Mix the washed rocket, tomatoes, gherkins and carrot in a salad bowl.

For the beer dressing, add the olive oil to a pot over a medium heat and sauté the shallot and thyme until the shallot is soft. Add the beer and reduce by half. On a high heat, this will take roughly 4–5 minutes. Then whisk in the remaining ingredients: honey, vinegar, mustard. Leave to simmer for 2 more minutes, then set aside.

With a nice hot pan on a high heat, add some oil and fry the beef. The faster you cook the beef the better as you don't want to overcook it. After 4–5 minutes cooking, add your broccoli and cashew nuts. Cook for 1 further minute.

Divide your salad into four bowls. Place some crispy potatoes around the salad and equal portions of the beef on top. Spoon the dressing on, then crumble the blue cheese or Parmesan on top.

# PASTA CAPRESE RIGATONI WITH PLUM TOMATOES & BUFFALO MOZZARELLA

SERVES 4

## INGREDIENTS

3 tsp olive oil, plus extra for drizzling

600g rigatoni

1 shallot

4 cloves of garlic

400g plum tomatoes, chopped

Salt, to season

100g broad beans, peeled and cooked

1 tsp chopped chives

8 basil leaves, chopped

100g cherry tomatoes, halved

2 avocados, chopped

2 buffalo mozzarella, diced

100g rocket

## METHOD

Bring a large pot of salted water to the boil. Add 1 teaspoon of olive oil to the water, then add the pasta. Cook for roughly 10 minutes. It should be al dente and not soft; otherwise the pasta will fall apart. Strain and return to the pot.

Heat another pan. Add 2 teaspoons of olive oil, then lightly sauté the shallot and garlic until soft, without allowing them to colour. This should take 2 minutes. Add your plum tomatoes and season well – as you know, tomatoes can be bland. Cook for 7 minutes, then blend with a hand blender or food processor and allow to cool. Once cool, add the broad beans and chives.

Mix your pasta with the sauce and add the chopped basil and cherry tomatoes. Place into four bowls, with the chopped avocado and diced mozzarella on top. Drizzle some olive oil on top, followed by a garnish of rocket leaves.

### ♨ VARIATIONS:
You can mix this pasta salad up by adding chicken or fresh chargrilled tuna. One of my favourite additions is chorizo.

# LEMON & THYME ROASTED CHICKEN, CHERRY TOMATO, MANGO, PARMESAN SHAVINGS & LIME & CHILLI YOGHURT

This is so simple but tasty and good.

SERVES 4

## INGREDIENTS

4 skinless chicken breasts, cut into strips

1 tsp fresh thyme

Juice and zest of 1 lemon

Juice and zest of 1 lime

Olive oil

500g mixed baby leaves

100g cherry tomatoes, halved

1 mango, peeled and sliced

Seeds of 1 pomegranate

50g Parmesan shavings

LIME & CHILLI DRESSING

200ml natural yoghurt

1 red chilli, deseeded and chopped

1 green chilli, deseeded and chopped

1 tsp chopped coriander

1 tsp chopped parsley

Juice and zest of 1 lime

## METHOD

First of all, marinate the chicken strips in the thyme and lemon and lime juices and zest. Put in a sealed container, preferably overnight, but for at least 1 hour. You want to maximise the flavours.

For the dressing, mix all the ingredients together. You could do this the day before.

Preheat the oven to 170°C.

Heat a griddle, add some oil and cook the chicken strips for 2 minutes on either side, then put in the oven for 8 minutes until cooked.

Lay out four bowls. Place your washed baby leaves in the bowl first, followed by some cherry tomatoes, mango and pomegranate seeds. Place the cooked chicken on top, then add your dressing, followed by Parmesan shavings.

❋TIP:
The best way to get the seeds from a pomegranate is to cut it in half and gently hit the back of the fruit – the seeds should pop out.

♨VARIATIONS:
Instead of Parmesan, you could add some feta, blue cheese or goats' cheese.

# STICKY TERIYAKI CHICKEN WITH MANGO & CORIANDER SALSA & BEANSPROUT SALAD

SERVES 4–6

## INGREDIENTS

4 large chicken breasts

3 tsp olive oil

1 tsp Cajun spice (optional)

70g soy sauce

70g honey

70g brown sugar

50ml pineapple juice

1 tsp cornflour

1 red pepper, diced

1 yellow pepper, diced

1 red onion, diced

10 button mushrooms, halved

1 tsp rapeseed oil

500g beansprouts

1 red chilli, finely sliced

1 bunch of coriander, chopped

MANGO SALSA

2 mangos, diced

1 tsp olive oil

Juice and zest of 1 lime

½ red chilli, deseeded and chopped

1 tsp chopped coriander

Salt

## METHOD

First of all, cut the chicken into large dice. You should get six pieces from each breast. Rub the diced chicken with the olive oil. If you like, add a small bit of Cajun spice for flavour. Leave to rest in the fridge for 1 hour.

To make the sauce, heat the soy sauce, honey, sugar and pineapple juice in a small saucepan over a high heat. Once the sauce boils, thicken it slightly using the cornflour. Leave to cool, then add to the chicken and marinate for a further 3 hours. The longer the chicken is marinated, the better the taste.

For the mango salsa, mix all the ingredients and taste for seasoning.

Thread the chicken on skewers along with your diced yellow and red peppers, onion and mushrooms. You can simply cook these in the oven, but they're even tastier if they are char-grilled first. If simply baking, preheat the oven to 180°C and cook for 10–12 minutes until the chicken is cooked. If char-grilling, preheat the oven, then add 1 teaspoon of rapeseed oil to a nice hot griddle pan and seal the skewers for two minutes on each side, finishing in the oven for 8–10 minutes.

Place on a plate, criss-crossed or whichever way you want. Garnish with your beansprouts, chilli and coriander. Serve the mango salsa on the side.

♨VARIATIONS:
You can try loads of different meats and fish: prawns, lamb, salmon and beef all work well.

# GOATS' CHEESE, BEETROOT & GREEN BEAN SALAD

There is plenty of good goats' cheese available. In Cork, we have two: Bluebell Falls and Ardsallagh.

SERVES 4

## INGREDIENTS

80g ciabatta (standard size roll)

Olive oil for drizzling

400g Ardsallagh goats' cheese

90g fresh breadcrumbs

20g rocket pesto (see p. 58)

50g flaked almonds

8 cherry tomatoes

Salt, to season

150g green beans, halved

300g baby leaves

200g cooked beetroot, diced

50ml hazelnut oil

## METHOD

Preheat the oven to 180°C.

Cut the ciabatta in half and then again down the middle, giving you four squares. Drizzle with olive oil and bake for 4 minutes until nice and crispy.

Cut four slices of goats' cheese, roughly 100 grams per serving. Place on top of the ciabatta. Mix the breadcrumbs with the pesto, then sprinkle on top of the goats' cheese. Bake in the oven for 8–10 minutes.

Toast the almonds until they get a golden colour.

Roast the cherry tomatoes with salt and olive oil until the skin cracks. Allow to cool.

Blanch the green beans in boiling salted water for 1 minute and refresh in ice-cold water.

In a bowl, mix your baby leaves, beetroot, green beans and crispy almonds. Dress with the hazelnut oil. Put a portion of salad on a plate with a piece of your goats' cheese ciabatta on top, some cherry tomatoes around the side, and if you have any pesto left over, drizzle some over the goats' cheese. Serve straight away!

# VEGETABLE & BARLEY BROTH

My white soda bread (see p. 25) is the perfect bread for this bowl of pure comfort food.
Dice the vegetables as small as you can for this soup.

 SERVES 8

## INGREDIENTS

100g barley

2 tsp rapeseed oil

2 cloves of garlic, chopped

4 sticks of celery, finely diced

1 medium onion, finely chopped

2 carrots, finely chopped

1 turnip, finely chopped

1 leek, finely chopped

1 large sweet potato, diced

2 litres vegetable stock

1 tsp cornflour (optional)

1 tsp chopped parsley

1 tsp chopped chives

## METHOD

Soak the barley overnight, just covering it with water.

To a nice large pot over a low heat, add your rapeseed oil, then the garlic, celery, onion, carrots, turnip and leek. Sauté for 4 minutes to release all the flavours without colouring.

Add the barley and sweet potato, then pour in your stock. Simmer for 35 minutes until the vegetables and barley are cooked.

If you would like your broth to be thicker, then mix a teaspoon of cornflour in a bowl with the same amount of stock, before adding to the soup, which has to be boiling when you do this, otherwise it will not thicken.

Add the fresh herbs when serving.

# SPICY CARROT & LENTIL SOUP

SERVES 6–8

## INGREDIENTS

200g red lentils

2 tsp olive oil

1kg carrots, peeled and chopped

1 medium onion, chopped

3 cloves of garlic, chopped

2 sticks of celery, peeled and chopped

1 leek, washed and chopped

2 tsp chilli flakes

1 tsp garam masala

1 tsp turmeric

1.5 litres vegetable stock

## METHOD

Cover the lentils in water and soak for 1 hour before using.

To a pot over a low heat, add the olive oil, then the carrots, onion, garlic, celery and leek. Sauté for 3 minutes until the vegetables are soft. Add your chilli flakes, garam masala and turmeric and continue to cook for 4 more minutes.

Drain the lentils, then add to the vegetables. Add the stock and cook for roughly 45 minutes on a medium heat. While it's cooking you should be able to smell the lovely flavours.

When it is cooked, blitz and pass through a sieve to make it smooth. If you like your soup chunky, don't use the sieve. Serve with brown bread (see p. 22). Beautiful!

# CHICKEN & NOODLE SOUP

SERVES 4

## INGREDIENTS

1 tsp olive oil

2 large chicken fillets

50ml vegetable oil

1 shallot, diced

20g fresh ginger, grated

1 tsp Thai green curry paste

500ml chicken stock

300ml coconut milk

2 lime leaves

150g egg noodles

1 carrot, finely sliced

1 courgette, finely sliced

1 red chilli, chopped

1 bunch of coriander, chopped

1 spring onion, sliced

1 small baby bok choi, sliced

Lime juice (optional)

## METHOD

Preheat the oven to 180°C.

To a hot griddle pan, add the olive oil and chargrill the chicken for 2 minutes on either side. Finish it off in the oven for 20 minutes. Once the chicken is cooked and cooled, thinly slice.

Heat the vegetable oil in a pan. Add the shallot and ginger and then the green curry paste. Cook gently for 2 minutes. Gently pour in your stock and coconut milk and add the lime leaves. If you don't have lime leaves, use the juice of half a lime. Bring to the boil, then leave to simmer for 10 minutes.

Meanwhile place the noodles in boiling hot water and cook for 2 minutes. Drain and separate evenly into four bowls with the sliced chicken.

To finish the soup, add the carrot and courgette and cook for a further 3 minutes. Then add the remaining ingredients: chilli, coriander, spring onion and bok choi. Taste for seasoning and add a squeeze of lime if it needs it.

Pour the soup over your chicken and noodles and serve. If the soup is too hot for your liking, you can add some crème fraîche or yoghurt.

# BALLYCOTTON CHUNKY SEAFOOD CHOWDER

We buy our fresh chowder mix from the boats of Ballycotton, right on our doorstep.
Lovely fresh fish! Most supermarkets have beautiful fresh fish.

SERVES 4

## INGREDIENTS

30g butter

1 small onion, diced

1 leek, finely chopped

1 carrot, finely chopped

2 sticks of celery, finely chopped

300ml white wine

400ml fresh fish stock (or made from stock cubes)

1 large potato, peeled and finely chopped

1 tsp cornflour, if needed

400g chowder mix

100g mussel meat

100g fresh squid rings

100g cooked prawns, peeled

200ml cream

1 tsp chopped parsley

Juice of 1 lemon

## METHOD

Heat a large pot and add your butter. When it has melted, add your onion, leek, carrot and celery. Cook for 3–5 minutes but do not allow to colour.

Add the white wine, bring to the boil, and allow to reduce by half. Then add the fish stock and diced potato. Once it comes to the boil, turn the heat down to a simmer. Most chowders use flour, but we do not as the potato provides starch. If you do not leave the sauce to reduce enough, it will not thicken. If that happens, add 1 teaspoon of cornflour mixed with cold water and stir into the chowder, but the sauce has to be boiling when you do this, otherwise it won't thicken.

Add the chowder mix and only allow to cook for 4 minutes. Then add the mussels, squid, prawns and cream. Leave to cook for 4 more minutes. Stir in the chopped parsley and a squeeze of lemon juice at the last minute.

Check for seasoning and serve with some bread and Bandon butter.

# ROAST RED PEPPER & TOMATO SOUP WITH CHEESE CROUTONS

SERVES 4—6

## INGREDIENTS

3 tsp olive oil

8 plum tomatoes, chopped

8 red peppers, deseeded and chopped

1 medium onion, chopped

4 cloves of garlic, chopped

20g fresh ginger, grated

2 tsp tomato paste

500g chopped tomatoes

500ml vegetable stock

1 bunch of basil

1 bunch of coriander

Lemon juice (optional)

White sugar (optional)

### CHEESE CROUTONS

3 slices of bread

1 tsp olive oil

10g butter

1 tsp dried parsley

1 tsp dried Parmesan dust

## METHOD

Heat a large pot. Add the olive oil, then sauté the plum tomatoes, peppers, onion, garlic and ginger. After about 5–7 minutes, when the vegetables are getting soft, add the tomato paste and cook for a further 2 minutes.

Add the chopped tomatoes and stock, and leave to simmer for 1 hour. The longer you cook this soup the more flavour you will get from the tomatoes. You could even leave it to cook slowly for 2 hours.

When the soup is ready, blitz with your fresh herbs and pass through a strainer. Taste for seasoning. If your soup is bitter, add lemon juice and some sugar to sweeten it up.

For the cheese croutons, preheat the oven to 180°C. Dice the bread into small cubes. Heat the olive oil and butter in a pan. When melted, add the bread and dried parsley and mix well with a spoon. Place onto a tray and cook in the oven for 12–14 minutes until nice and crispy. Sprinkle your Parmesan over the hot croutons and allow to cool.

Pour the soup into bowls with the cheese croutons on top. A dash of pesto would be nice too, if you have it.

# PUMPKIN SOUP WITH FRESH SAGE & TOASTED PUMPKIN SEEDS

SERVES 8

## INGREDIENTS

1kg pumpkin, peeled, deseeded and chopped into medium-size chunks

150ml olive oil

200g carrots, peeled and diced

1 large sweet potato, sliced

3 cloves of garlic, chopped

1 medium onion, sliced

20g fresh ginger, peeled and chopped

1 tsp ground cumin

1 tsp salt

2 litres vegetable stock

50g pumpkin seeds

1 tsp chopped sage

100ml cream

## METHOD

Preheat the oven to 160°C.

Mix the pumpkin with 100ml of olive oil and roast for 30–40 minutes until cooked but not coloured. Leave the oven on when it's done.

Meanwhile, add 50ml of olive oil to a large pot on a low heat and start sautéing your carrots, sweet potato, garlic, onion, ginger and cumin. Season with salt to taste. It will take about 5 minutes to extract the flavours.

Add the roasted pumpkin to the pot, then the vegetable stock, and allow to cook for 30 minutes.

While the soup is cooking, toast your pumpkin seeds in the oven for 3–5 minutes.

When the soup is ready, blitz with a hand blender or use a food processor. Check for seasoning and consistency. If it's too thick, add more water, but it should be right! Add your chopped sage at the end. To serve, ladle the soup into a bowl, spoon in some cream and sprinkle some pumpkin seeds on top.

✻TIP:
You really need to baste the pumpkin while it's roasting so it does not dry out.

♨VARIATION:
You could swap the sage with red chilli for a hotter soup. Add the chilli when you are cooking the vegetables.

MAIN COURSES

# DAD'S BACON & CABBAGE

One Sunday, Dad said, 'Make dinner – you're supposed to be a chef!' I had just turned seventeen, so I said,
'Fine, I'll make bacon and cabbage, but I will fry the cabbage and bake the potatoes in the oven for mash.'
Dad thought this was the funniest thing in the world – he was so used to Mam boiling everything!
(There's nothing wrong with that, but I just wanted to make it a bit fancier.)
In the end, it became one of Dad's favourite dinners.

SERVES 4–6

## INGREDIENTS

1.5kg bacon loin

1 stick of celery (optional)

1 onion (optional)

6 large carrots, sliced, plus
1 roughly cut (optional)

6 large potatoes

125g butter

200ml cream

Salt and pepper, to season

25g honey

1 tsp chopped chives

### GLAZE FOR BACON

50g honey

50g brown sugar

50g mustard

### FRIED CABBAGE

100g butter

1 medium onion, diced

4 cloves of garlic, chopped

1 sprig of thyme, chopped

100g streaky bacon rashers, cut
into pieces

1 head green cabbage

## METHOD

Put your bacon into a pot of water. Add 1 roughly cut celery stick, onion and carrot. (These are optional, but will add to the flavour.) Once the bacon comes to the boil, leave to simmer for 1 hour and 20 minutes. While the bacon is cooking combine all the ingredients for the glaze.

Preheat the oven to 170°C.

Once the bacon is cooked, remove it from the pot. Remove the vegetables from the stock also and place on a baking tray with the bacon on top. This prevents the bacon from sticking to the bottom of the tray. Keep the bacon stock – you need it for the cabbage. You can trim a small bit of fat from the top of the bacon if you wish. Rub the glaze onto the bacon. Put it in the oven and cook for 20–30 minutes until golden brown.

With a small knife, pierce the skin of the potatoes and wrap in foil. They will take 1 hour to cook at least. Once cooked, allow to cool a little, then cut lengthwise, scoop out the flesh and mash. Add 100g of butter, followed by the cream. Season with salt and pepper to taste.

Cook the carrots in salted water for 20 minutes. When they are cooked they should be tender but holding their shape. Strain and add 25g of butter and the honey. Season with salt and put into a bowl. Sprinkle with the chopped chives.

**PARSLEY SAUCE**

300ml milk

2 tsp cornflour

½ tsp mustard

½ tsp dried parsley

For the famous cabbage, melt the butter in a pot and fry the onion, garlic, thyme and streaky bacon for about 3 minutes on a low heat. You don't want them to colour. Shred the cabbage as finely as you can. You want the cabbage to cook fast and keep its green colour. Don't worry, it will still be cooked. Add the cabbage to the onion and bacon. After 2 minutes, add 100ml of your bacon stock. Leave to cook for 3 more minutes, until there is no liquid left in the pot.

Now for the parsley sauce. Bring the milk to the boil. Mix the cornflour with 1 teaspoon of water and add this to the milk just before it boils. Add the mustard and parsley and cook for 2 minutes on a very low heat. Check for seasoning. If it gets too thick, add some more water.

To serve, place the bacon on a board or plate in the middle of the table, with the potatoes, carrots and cabbage on the side and the parsley sauce in a sauce boat.

♨VARIATION:

As the years went by we added bacon ribs (bodis). I personally love bodis. You can buy them in any local butcher's. Cut them into two little racks and cook with the bacon – a nice extra touch on the side.

# THE CORKONIAN BEEF BURGER WITH GUBBEEN CHEESE, FAT FRIES & PINK SAUCE

SERVES 4

## INGREDIENTS

FAT FRIES

8 large potatoes

3 tsp rapeseed oil

2 cloves of garlic, chopped

1 tsp Cajun spice (optional)

BURGER

2 tsp rapeseed oil

1 shallot, diced small

2 cloves of garlic, chopped

700g beef mince

1 tsp Dijon mustard

1 egg yolk

Salt and pepper

Gubbeen cheese

4 brioche buns

Shredded iceberg lettuce

1 large beef tomato, sliced

Onion jam (see p. 152)

8 pieces streaky bacon, cooked

Sliced gherkins

PINK SAUCE

100g mayonnaise

100g ketchup

1 tsp Worchester sauce

## METHOD

Preheat the oven to 180°C.

Cut the potatoes into wedges, put in a pot of salted water and bring to the boil. Simmer for 5 minutes – you want them still slightly hard – then drain and run cold water over them until they are completely cold.

Put the chips in a bowl and mix them with the rapeseed oil (making sure you cover all the chips), the chopped garlic and the Cajun spice (if using). Place on a baking tray and put in the oven. It usually takes 25 minutes to get a nice crispy chip. Give them a good shake while cooking so they get an even colour all over.

For the burger, add 2 teaspoons of rapeseed oil to a pot and sauté the shallot and garlic over a low heat without allowing them to colour. This will take 2 minutes. Leave to cool. In a bowl, mix the beef with the mustard, egg yolk and salt and pepper to season. Add the cooled shallot and garlic. Make four evenly sized patties and allow to rest for 30 minutes.

For the sauce – as we call it in Cork, 'pink sauce' – just mix all the ingredients together.

In a hot pan, fry your burger for at least 2 minutes on each side. Then cook in the oven for 15 minutes and leave to rest for 2 minutes. Just note: your burger will shrink a small bit during the cooking. After it has rested, put a nice slice of your Gubbeen cheese on top of your burger and put it back in the oven until the cheese melts.

To serve, toast your brioche buns. Put some shredded lettuce and a slice of beef tomato, followed by 1 tablespoon of onion jam on one half of the bun. Place the burger and melted cheese on the other half of the bun, followed by the gherkin and bacon slices. Leave it open as it looks nicer, and there's your Corkonian burger! Serve with the fat fries and a bowl of pink sauce on the side.

❄TIP:
Ask the butcher to give you beef chuck or brisket for the mince. These make a good quality burger.

# FRIED BUTTERMILK CHICKEN STRIPS WITH CRISPY SWEET POTATO CUBES & A ROAST GARLIC AIOLI

A lovely dish for the summer, really tasty and easy to make.

SERVES 4

## INGREDIENTS

4 chicken fillets, cut into strips
500ml buttermilk
Juice and zest of 1 lime
5g fresh ginger, grated
150g plain flour
75g porridge oats
2 tsp Cajun spice
1 tsp garlic powder
1 red chilli
1 lime, cut into wedges

### SWEET POTATO CUBES
100g Cajun spice
3 cloves of garlic, chopped
2 sprigs of fresh rosemary
6 large sweet potatoes, peeled and diced
3 tsp rapeseed oil
Salt and pepper

### ROAST GARLIC AIOLI
1 head of garlic
300g mayonnaise
1 tsp chopped chives
Juice and zest of ½ lime

## METHOD

Cut the chicken into strips. I usually get five strips from a fillet. Mix with the buttermilk, the lime juice and zest and the grated ginger. Marinate overnight.

For the aioli, preheat the oven to 170°C. Wrap the garlic head in tinfoil and roast in the oven for 40 minutes. Once cooked and cooled, squeeze out the insides and mix with the mayonnaise, chives and lime juice and zest.

For the sweet potato cubes, mix the Cajun spice, chopped garlic and rosemary in a bowl with the sweet potato. Add the rapeseed oil and mix, making sure the oil has touched all of the potato. Place on a baking tray and cook for 30 minutes. The potatoes should be soft but still holding their cube shape. Season to taste with salt and pepper.

For the chicken crumb, mix the flour, porridge oats, Cajun spice and garlic powder together. Take your chicken pieces out of the marinade and dip them one by one into the crumb, making sure all the chicken is coated.

Cook your chicken in a deep-fat fryer at 175°C until golden brown. Remove and drain on kitchen paper. This will take 5 minutes. If you don't have a fryer, then it's the old-fashioned way: put a good amount of vegetable oil into a deep pot and bring to the correct temperature using a thermometer, then cook as you would in a fryer.

Sprinkle the chicken with some chopped fresh red chilli and serve with lime wedges, sweet potatoes and garlic aioli on the side.

# POT-ROASTED MIDLETON LAMB SHANK WITH SPICED RED CABBAGE, HONEY-ROASTED CARROTS & MINT SAUCE

SERVES 4

## INGREDIENTS

2 tsp rapeseed oil

4 lamb shanks, roughly 300g each

Salt and pepper

1 stick of celery

1 carrot, diced

1 onion, diced

1 bulb of fennel, diced

2 tsp tomato paste

2 tsp flour (optional)

2 litres lamb stock (you can also use chicken stock)

3 sprigs of rosemary

3 sprigs of thyme

2 star anise

### MINT SAUCE

1 bunch of mint, chopped

½ bunch of flat-leaf parsley, chopped

1 clove of garlic, chopped

1 tsp caster sugar

70ml boiling water

70ml vinegar

## METHOD

Preheat the oven to 170°C, then heat a large casserole pot over a high heat. Add the rapeseed oil, followed by the lamb shanks seasoned with salt and pepper. Once browned, remove the shanks from the pot.

Add the celery, carrot, onion and fennel to the same pot and cook for 3 minutes. Then add the tomato paste followed by the flour (if using) and mix. The flour is optional – it's just to make your sauce nice and thick.

Pour in your lamb stock, and add the rosemary, thyme and star anise. Stir well and make sure there isn't anything stuck to the bottom of the pot. Return the lamb to the pot and cook for 3 hours or until the meat is ready to fall off the bone. The bigger the lamb shanks, the longer they will take to cook.

Remove the lamb and strain the stock. Put the stock into a pot and reduce by two-thirds – this can be used as a sauce for your lamb.

For the cabbage, heat a large pot on a medium heat and add 2 teaspoons of rapeseed oil. Add the cabbage and sauté for 3 minutes. Add the sugar, cinnamon, nutmeg, bay leaves and five spice and cook for another 3 minutes. Pour in all your liquids – red wine, chicken stock and red-wine vinegar. Bring to the boil, then turn down the heat and allow to simmer on a low heat for 35–40 minutes until cooked.

## SPICED RED CABBAGE

2 tsp rapeseed oil

1 whole red cabbage, sliced

50g brown sugar

1 cinnamon stick

Pinch of nutmeg

2 bay leaves

1 tsp five spice

300ml red wine

500ml chicken stock

150ml red-wine vinegar

## HONEY-ROASTED CARROTS

6 large carrots, cut into large dice

50g brown sugar

50g honey (warm)

20g butter, melted

1 sprig of freshly chopped thyme

For the mint sauce, mix the mint, parsley and garlic. Add the sugar, followed by the boiling water. Give it a whisk, then add the vinegar. Done.

Boil a pot of salted water and cook the diced carrots for 7–8 minutes. At this point they should still have a bite and not be fully cooked. Strain them and place on a baking tray. Mix the sugar, honey, butter and thyme, and coat the carrots, ensuring they are well covered. Roast in the oven for 15 minutes until they are nice and sticky and fully cooked.

To plate up, arrange the cabbage and carrots first, with the lamb and stock sauce on top. Follow with your mint sauce on the side.

# SPICY VEGETABLE LASAGNE WITH GOATS' CHEESE TOASTIES

SERVES 4

## INGREDIENTS

2 tsp rapeseed oil

4 cloves of garlic, chopped

2 carrots, diced

1 squash, diced

3 red peppers, diced

2 aubergines, diced

2 courgettes, diced

2 tsp Cajun spice

500g spinach

200g kidney beans

12 lasagne sheets

200g smoked cheddar, grated

### TOMATO SAUCE

1 tsp rapeseed oil

1 red onion, diced

4 cloves of garlic, chopped

½ red chilli, diced

1 tsp tomato paste

600g chopped tomatoes

1 tsp chopped basil

1 tsp chopped coriander

### WHITE SAUCE

30g butter

3 tsp plain flour

350ml milk

1 tsp chopped parsley

## METHOD

Add the rapeseed oil to a non-stick pan, and fry the garlic, followed by the carrots, squash, red peppers, aubergines, courgettes and the Cajun spice. Fry for roughly 5 minutes; you do not want to fully cook the vegetables. Then add the spinach, mix through and set aside.

Next, the tomato sauce. Add the rapeseed oil to a pot and lightly sauté the onion, garlic and red chilli. Then add the tomato paste and chopped tomatoes, cooking on a low heat for 30 minutes. You want your sauce to be nice and thick, a jam-like consistency. Once the sauce is cooked, add the chopped basil and coriander, then add the kidney beans, followed by the vegetables.

For the white sauce, melt the butter, then add the flour. Using a wooden spoon, cook the roux for 2 minutes. Add the milk slowly and whisk to make sure there are no lumps. Once it comes to the boil reduce to a low heat and cook slowly for a further 5 minutes. Add the parsley at the end.

Preheat the oven to 170°C. Assemble your lasagne in a 20 cm rectangular baking dish: a layer of vegetables first, followed by a layer of lasagne sheets. Repeat this two more times. Then pour your white sauce on top and sprinkle the cheddar cheese over the sauce. Cook for 40–45 minutes until the pasta is soft and the cheese is golden brown.

For the toasties, cut the baguette into five slices. Spread with the goats' cheese and cook for 6 minutes in the oven. You

## GOATS' CHEESE TOASTIES

2 large baguettes
200g soft goats' cheese

could sprinkle chopped walnuts on top to give a bit more of a crunch.

Once the lasagne is ready, spoon onto a plate. A nice rustic salad to lift the plate with colour would be beautiful. Serve your toasties on the side.

❊TIP:
A 'rustic salad' could mean anything – whatever you have lying around in the fridge. It does not have to be a perfect salad, meaning you could add anything to it!

# GRILLED SALMON FILLET WITH PUMPKIN SEED & SUN-DRIED TOMATO CRUST, SQUASH PURÉE & BRAISED BABY POTATOES

*SERVES 4*

## INGREDIENTS

1 small butternut squash

4 tsp rapeseed oil

1 clove of garlic, finely chopped

1 sprig of thyme, finely chopped

100g butter

150g fresh breadcrumbs

100g sun-dried tomatoes, chopped

20g pumpkin seeds

20g flaked almonds

1 tsp chopped parsley

4 salmon fillets (*c.* 200g each)

8 cherry tomatoes

Salt, to season

### BRAISED BABY POTATOES

12 baby potatoes

1 tsp turmeric

2 sprigs of rosemary

Salt, to season

## METHOD

Preheat the oven to 170°C. Cut the squash in half lengthways, discarding the seeds, and place on a baking tray, flesh side up. Mix 2 teaspoons of rapeseed oil with the garlic and thyme, and rub onto the squash. Cover with parchment paper and then tinfoil and bake for 30–35 minutes until soft and cooked. When your squash is nicely soft, scoop out the flesh and blend with 50g of butter until it is a nice, smooth, silky purée, with no lumps.

For the crust, mix the breadcrumbs, sun-dried tomatoes, pumpkin seeds and flaked almonds together with the chopped parsley and 50g of melted butter.

Now for the tricky part, the baby potatoes. You will need an apple corer for this. Push the corer halfway up the baby potatoes, and with a small knife cut away the outside of the potato up to the level of the top of the corer. When you push the potato out from the corer using your finger, your potato should look like a mushroom. Repeat with all 12 potatoes, then put in a pan and cover with water. Add the turmeric, rosemary and a pinch of salt. Just so you know, the turmeric will turn the potato yellow. Bring to the boil and simmer for roughly 15 minutes until cooked.

Heat a griddle pan over a high heat. Add 1 teaspoon of rapeseed oil, then turn down the heat slightly. Rub your salmon with a little oil and griddle, lengthways first and then sideways to get the nice cross-hatch pattern. Place on a tray, put your crust on top and bake in the preheated oven for 10–12 minutes until cooked through.

Drizzle some rapeseed oil and sprinkle some sea salt over the tomatoes and roast until the skin cracks. This should take 3 minutes.

Now your hard work has paid off. Plate up with the purée on the bottom, the salmon on top, and baby potatoes and tomatoes to the side. You could also add some garden peas for more colour.

# COTTAGE PIE WITH SMOKED APPLEWOOD CHEDDAR MASH

Every family has their own version of this old-time favourite. My kids love this pie and so do their parents.

SERVES 6–8

## INGREDIENTS

800g mince

Rapeseed oil

Salt and pepper, to season

1 medium onion, finely diced

3 cloves of garlic, finely diced

2 sprigs of thyme, picked and finely chopped

2 sticks of celery, finely diced

3 carrots, finely diced

10 button mushrooms, finely sliced

2 tsp tomato paste

600ml beef stock

### CHEDDAR MASH

6 large baking potatoes

120g butter

150g Applewood cheddar, grated

3 spring onions, finely sliced

## METHOD

In a large pot, fry the mince in some rapeseed oil until nice and brown. Make sure you season with salt and pepper – mince can be bland. Add the onion, garlic and thyme and cook for 2 more minutes. Then add the celery, carrots and mushrooms and cook for a further 5 minutes. You are allowing all the flavours from the vegetables and meat to marry into something tasty.

Add the tomato paste and cook for another minute. Then add your beef stock and allow to cook slowly for 25–30 minutes until the beef is tender and the sauce has thickened. Once ready, pour into a casserole dish and leave to cool for at least 1 hour before adding the mash.

Peel the potatoes and cut in half. Put in salted water on a high heat. Once the potatoes come to the boil, turn the heat down and simmer for 20–25 minutes until cooked.

Preheat the oven to 170°C.

When the potatoes are cooked, strain the water and mash the potatoes until there are no lumps. Add the butter, cheese and spring onions, and season to taste. Spoon on top of the cooked mince and spread evenly. Cook for 30 minutes until the surface of the mash is golden brown.

VARIATION:
You can make a shepherd's pie by swapping the beef with lamb.

# CHICKEN CURRY

A nice and simple curry that can be made a day in advance.
I have added a couple of extra touches so you can put on a spread for curry night.

SERVES 4

## INGREDIENTS

4 chicken breasts, diced

Rapeseed oil

1 red onion, diced

1 red pepper, diced

5 cloves of garlic, finely chopped

1 red chilli, chopped

10g fresh ginger, grated

½ tsp ground coriander

2 tsp Madras powder

½ tsp turmeric

800g chopped tomatoes

100g beansprouts

1 red pepper, sliced

1 spring onion, diced

1 tsp chopped coriander

Naan bread

Raita (see p. 66)

### RICE

300g long-grain rice

1 tsp ground turmeric

Pinch of salt

2 cloves of garlic, chopped

1 small carrot, grated

2 tsp blended sesame oil

1 tsp chopped chives

## METHOD

Sauté the chicken in a hot pan in a little rapeseed oil. Once coloured, remove from the pan and place onto a baking tray. To the same pan, add the onion, pepper, garlic, chilli, ginger, ground coriander, Madras powder and turmeric, and cook for 3 minutes over a low heat to release all the flavours from the spices.

Add the chicken back into the pan and allow to cook for a further minute. Then add the chopped tomatoes and leave to slowly cook for 20 minutes over a low heat.

Add your rice and turmeric to salted water. Once it comes to the boil, reduce the heat and allow to cook for 12 minutes, then strain off the water. Fry the garlic and carrot in the sesame oil for 30 seconds – you don't want to overcook the carrot. Add to the rice, along with the chopped chives.

Mix the beansprouts, red pepper, spring onion and coriander together. This is your garnish for the top of the curry.

Warm the naan bread. You need bread for soaking up the curry sauce! To serve, put everything into separate dishes and garnish the curry with the beansprout mix. As you can see from my pictures, I use a curry bowl with the rice, raita and naan bread all to the side.

# BLACKENED TURKEY TACOS, TOMATO & BEAN SALSA, AVOCADO & SOUR CREAM

**SERVES 4—6**

## INGREDIENTS

600g turkey breast, cut in strips

2 tsp Cajun spice

Pinch of sea salt

3 tsp rapeseed oil, plus extra for griddling

12 small taco shells

½ iceberg lettuce, shredded

Guacamole (see p. 53)

200ml sour cream

50g smoked cheddar, grated

### SALSA

100g refried (pinto) beans

100g sun-dried tomatoes in oil

Juice of 1 lime

1 tsp chopped basil

1 tsp chopped coriander

## METHOD

Place your turkey meat in a bowl. Add the Cajun spice, salt and oil. Mix well. Cover with cling film and leave the turkey to absorb the spices for at least 30 minutes.

For the salsa, simply mix the beans, tomatoes, lime juice, basil and coriander, and leave to the side.

Preheat the oven to 180°C.

To cook the turkey, I like to chargrill. Heat up the griddle, add some oil and grill the turkey on each side until cooked. This can also be done on a barbecue or in a frying pan.

Warm the taco shells in the oven for 3 minutes.

To serve, divide the shredded lettuce among the taco shells. Top with a spoonful of guacamole followed by some cooked turkey. Then add some salsa, a large dollop of sour cream and sprinkle your grated cheddar on top.

♨ VARIATIONS:
Use BBQ beans instead of the salsa.
You could also use chicken or salmon instead of turkey.

# BEEF SHORT RIB IN RED WINE WITH ROAST GARLIC MASH & PICKLED ONION SAUCE

This is a lovely winter dish when served with a loaf of crispy bread and full-fat Bandon butter for soaking up the sauce. Cooking meat on the bone is such a natural way of getting all the flavours from it. Your local butcher will have short ribs. Ask for four thick-cut, meaty beef short ribs weighing roughly 400g each.

SERVES 4

## INGREDIENTS

4 beef short ribs
Salt and pepper, to season
1 onion, chopped
6 cloves of garlic, chopped
1 carrot, chopped
1 tsp tomato paste
3 sprigs of rosemary
1 litre beef stock
600ml red wine

ROAST GARLIC MASH
6 baking potatoes
1 whole garlic bulb
80g butter
100ml milk
1 tsp chopped chives
Salt, to season

PICKLED ONION SAUCE
100g forest mushrooms
1 small onion, diced
2 sprigs of thyme, chopped
1 tsp rapeseed oil
200g silverskin onions
250ml red wine

## METHOD

Preheat the oven to 170°C.

Heat a large ovenproof casserole dish or deep tray over a high heat. Season the meat with salt and pepper, then fry until a nice brown colour all over.

Once brown, remove from the casserole dish/tray, then fry the onion, garlic and carrot in the fat that's left over from the meat. Add the tomato paste and rosemary and cook for a further 3 minutes.

Put your short ribs back into the casserole dish and add your stock and wine. Bring to the boil, then put in the oven and cook for at least 3 hours until the meat is tender and ready to fall away from the bone.

For the mash, pierce the skin of the potatoes, then wrap in tinfoil. Bake in the oven for 1 hour until nice and soft. These should go in to the oven an hour before the meat is cooked.

Wrap the whole garlic bulb in tinfoil and roast in the oven for 40 minutes. Once cooked, allow to cool, squeeze out the garlic and chop. When the potatoes are also cooked, cut in half lengthwise and scoop out the flesh when slightly cooled. Mash this, then add the butter and milk followed by the chives and garlic. Add salt to taste.

Sauté the mushrooms, diced onion and thyme in the rapeseed oil over a medium heat until soft. Add the silverskin onions and red wine and heat through. Leave to completely reduce down until there are barely 2 teaspoons of liquid left in the pot.

Once the short ribs are cooked, remove from the dish. Put the liquid from the casserole dish through a strainer, then add to the pickled onion sauce and leave to reduce down to the consistency you want.

Serve the short ribs on the mash and pour the sauce over the top.

✿TIP:
You can buy silverskin pickled onions in any local supermarket, but make sure you strain all the vinegar from the onions before adding them.

# CLONAKILTY CHICKEN SUPREME WITH SWEETCORN PURÉE, SPROUTING BROCCOLI & CRUSHED BABY POTATOES

'Supreme' means that the chicken is on the bone with its skin.
Try to use local Cork chicken – we have plenty in the county!

SERVES 4

## INGREDIENTS

4 chicken breasts, with skin
Salt, to season
Rapeseed oil

CRUSHED POTATOES
600g baby potatoes
1 tsp rapeseed oil
100g pancetta, diced
2 cloves of garlic, chopped
½ red onion, diced
1 tsp chopped parsley
1 tsp chopped chives

SWEETCORN PURÉE
300g frozen sweetcorn
300ml vegetable stock
1 clove of garlic, peeled
1 sprig of fresh thyme
30g butter

BROCCOLI
400g stem broccoli
20g butter, melted
20g flaked almonds, toasted
Salt and pepper, to season

## METHOD

Preheat the oven to 180°C.

Season the chicken on both sides. Then heat a pan, nice and hot. Add a little rapeseed oil and cook the chicken for 2 minutes on either side, skin side down first. Place onto a tray and cook in the oven for roughly 20–25 minutes.

While the chicken is roasting, cook your baby potatoes in salted water. After 20 minutes the potatoes should be cooked. Strain and crush with a masher.

Add 1 teaspoon of rapeseed oil to a pan and fry the pancetta, garlic and onion. Then add your parsley and chives. Mix with the crushed potatoes using a wooden spoon.

Put your sweetcorn in a pot with the stock, garlic and thyme. Bring to the boil and leave to simmer until the sweetcorn is soft and tender. Strain the sweetcorn, keeping the cooking liquid, and blend the sweetcorn with some of this liquid until smooth. Add the butter, stir until melted through, then season with salt to taste. Keep warm.

Put on a pot of salted water for the broccoli. Once the water comes to the boil, blanch the broccoli for 2 minutes and then remove. Melt your butter in a pan, add the toasted almonds and the broccoli, and mix together. Season to taste.

To serve, spoon the sweetcorn purée in the middle of the plate. Surround with the crushed baby potatoes. Sit the chicken on the purée, with the broccoli and almonds on top.

# MONKFISH SCAMPI, PEA PURÉE, LEMON AIOLI & PEA SHOOTS

Make the aioli the night before if you can. The mayonnaise will infuse with the lemon and garlic flavours.

SERVES 4

## INGREDIENTS

275g plain flour, plus extra for dusting

150g cornflour

12g salt, plus extra to serve

1 pint 'Friar Weisse' beer

5g turmeric

100g butter

1 shallot, finely diced

1 clove of garlic, chopped

200g peas

4 monkfish tails (180g each)

Lemon juice, to serve

LEMON AIOLI

150g mayonnaise

4 cloves of garlic, chopped

Juice and zest of 1 lemon

1 tsp chopped chives

❋TIP:
Don't use light mayonnaise – it takes away from the flavour and might split.

## METHOD

First make your batter. Place the flour, cornflour, salt, beer and turmeric together in a bowl and blitz with a hand blender. Leave to rest for 30 minutes.

To make the aioli, put the mayonnaise in a bowl, followed by the garlic, lemon and chives. Whisk together and then refrigerate.

Preheat your deep-fat fryer to 180°C. If you don't have a fryer, put enough vegetable oil to cover the scampi into a deep pot and bring to the same temperature, using a thermometer to check.

In a pot on the hob, melt the butter and sauté your shallot and garlic until soft, but not allowing them to colour. Add the peas and cook for a further 4 minutes. Once cooked, blitz in a food processor. If you want a fine purée, pass through a sieve using a spoon. Keep warm.

Cut the monkfish in four lengthways. This will give you four chunky strips. Dust with flour, dip into the batter until fully coated and cook until nice and crispy. This should take 3–4 minutes. Place the cooked monkfish on a tray with a paper napkin to soak off any grease.

To serve, put the pea purée on the plate first, with the fish on top. As you can see from the picture I garnished the dish with pea shoots. You can serve the aioli on the side. My fat fries (see p. 112) would be a perfect addition. To finish, add a squeeze of lemon juice and sea salt. I personally like vinegar, so that's also an option.

# HONEY-ROASTED SKEAGHANORE WEST CORK DUCK BREAST, ROOT VEGETABLE SALAD, PEARL BARLEY & BLACKCURRANT SAUCE

When I was working in the Woodstock in Ennis, I was asked to enter the Euro-Toques Young Chef of the Year competition. I was the only entrant from Munster. There were four of us in the final and this was my main course. Just so you know, in the dish in the photograph I added extras like burnt orange, sprout leaves and caramelised apple to show you the dish I made nearly sixteen years ago.

SERVES 4

## INGREDIENTS

Rapeseed oil

2 carrots, diced

1 small turnip, diced

1 small celeriac, diced

½ butternut squash, diced

Salt and pepper, to season

50g honey, plus extra to glaze

30g brown sugar

50g butter

2 sprigs of thyme, chopped

2 cooked beetroot, cut into wedges

4 duck breasts (220g each)

BARLEY

200g pearl barley

500ml vegetable stock

1 sprig of rosemary, chopped

1 clove of garlic, chopped

1 tsp chopped chives

Lemon juice

## METHOD

Make the sauce first. You can make this the day before, and it does taste better the next day. Place the red wine and thyme in a pan. Bring to the boil and reduce by half. Add your stock and again reduce by half. Then add the jam and whisk in the butter. This will give the sauce a nice shine. Finally, pass the sauce through a strainer.

Preheat the oven to 180°C.

Heat a frying pan over a medium heat. Once hot, add some rapeseed oil and sauté the carrots, turnip, celeriac and butternut squash until coloured. Season with salt and pepper. Remove the vegetables from the pan and place onto a baking tray.

In the same pan, mix the honey, brown sugar, butter and thyme. Once melted together, pour over the vegetables and mix well. Roast for 20 minutes until cooked, giving them a stir every 5 minutes. When your vegetables are cooked, add your cooked beetroot and mix. Put back in the oven to just warm the beetroot through.

Place the barley into a pot with the stock, rosemary and garlic. Bring to the boil and cook for 20–25 minutes. The

## BLACKCURRANT SAUCE

150ml red wine

1 sprig of thyme, chopped

150ml chicken stock

3 tsp blackcurrant jam

20g butter, diced (cold)

barley should be soft. Strain and leave to cool on a tray. Once cool, add the chopped chives with a squeeze of lemon juice.

Score the duck skin in a criss-cross pattern, and season with sea salt. Fry in a hot pan, skin side down, for 4 minutes. You want to render most of the fat. Turn onto the other side and cook for a further 2 minutes. Place onto an ovenproof tray, brush with honey and finish cooking for 6 minutes in the oven. Once cooked, leave to rest for 3 minutes. Then cut lengthways into two pieces.

To serve, place the vegetables in the centre of the plate, with a piece of duck on either side, and pour over your sauce. Sprinkle the pearl barley on top of the vegetables.

# HAKE FILLET, CANNELLINI BEAN, TOMATO & CHORIZO STEW WITH LIME CRÈME FRAÎCHE

This is an easy and classy dish, and another one of those where an accompanying loaf of bread won't go astray.

SERVES 4

## INGREDIENTS

Rapeseed oil

200g chorizo sausage, peeled and diced

1 baby shallot, diced

3 cloves of garlic, finely chopped

200g cannellini beans, cooked

600g chopped tomatoes

600g baby spinach

1 tsp chopped coriander

1 tsp chopped chives

Salt and pepper, to season

4 hake fillets (200g each)

Knob of butter

### LIME CRÈME FRAÎCHE

150ml yoghurt

Juice and zest of 1 lime

1 tsp chopped chives

## METHOD

Preheat the oven to 180°C.

Heat 1 teaspoon of rapeseed oil in a saucepan over a medium heat and sauté your chorizo, diced shallot and garlic for roughly 3 minutes to extract all the flavours from the sausage. Add the cannellini beans, followed by the chopped tomatoes and allow to slowly cook for roughly 10–12 minutes. To finish your stew, add the baby spinach, coriander and chives. Set aside, but keep warm. Taste and season before serving.

Heat a non-stick pan, add some rapeseed oil, and fry the hake fillets, skin side down, for 1 minute. Make sure your pan is hot, otherwise the fish will stick. When you turn the fish over, add a knob of butter and cook for 1 more minute, then season with salt and pepper. Place on a tray and cook in the oven for 8–10 minutes until the fish is cooked. It should be firm to touch.

For the lime crème fraîche, just mix all the ingredients together. If you want to add some heat to the sauce, add a few crushed pink peppercorns.

To serve, place your tomato stew in a bowl, with the fish on top. Drizzle your crème fraîche all over and add edible flowers for some bright colours.

♨VARIATION:
There is an ocean of fish that works with this dish: monkfish, cod, sea bass, turbot and plaice. Now there's some choice.

# PAN-FRIED FILLET STEAK WITH BABY SPINACH, FOREST MUSHROOMS, ONION JAM & TARRAGON BUTTER

If you want to impress, this is your show-stopper. I personally love rib-eye steak. A lot of people get turned off with the marble of fat in the centre, but that bit of fat makes the steak all the better! However, the fillet is the king of steaks.

SERVES 4

## INGREDIENTS

4 West Cork fillet steaks (200g each)

Salt and pepper, to season

Rapeseed oil

2 sprigs of rosemary

3 cloves of garlic, crushed

20g butter

ONION JAM

20g butter

3 red onions, sliced

2 sprigs of thyme, picked and chopped

20g caster sugar

300ml red wine

50ml port

MUSHROOMS AND SPINACH

1 banana shallot, diced

3 cloves of garlic, chopped

Rapeseed oil

300g mixed mushrooms, sliced

3 spring onions, sliced

1 tsp chopped chives

300g baby spinach

## METHOD

First for the onion jam, which can be made the day before. Melt the butter in a large pot. Add the onions and the thyme, and cook slowly over a low heat for 10 minutes. Add the sugar, wine and port. (If you don't have port to hand, you can just use 350ml of red wine.) Allow to cook, uncovered, for at least 25–30 minutes, stirring occasionally. When ready, the liquid should be reduced by about two-thirds. Check for taste, and if you find it's not sweet enough, add a little more sugar.

For the tarragon butter, mix the chopped tarragon and garlic with the butter. Using a piping bag with a star nozzle, pipe the butter into roughly 10 gram portions and put in the fridge. This can also be done the day before.

Preheat the oven to 170°C. Season your steaks with salt and pepper. To a nice hot pan, add some rapeseed oil, followed by your steaks and the rosemary and garlic. Allow the beef to seal for 2 minutes, then turn the steak and add the butter to the pan. Allow to cook for a further 2 minutes. Keep basting the steak: this will get you a lovely colour and add more flavour. If you do not seal and baste the meat properly it will take longer to cook. Finish the steaks in the oven. For medium, cook for roughly 10 minutes; for medium rare, 5 minutes; and for well done, 20 minutes. Allow to rest for 3 minutes after cooking.

## TARRAGON BUTTER

50g tarragon, chopped

3 cloves of garlic, chopped

100g butter, soft

To cook the vegetables, get a pan nice and hot. Sauté the shallot and garlic in some rapeseed oil, followed by the mushrooms. Cook for 2 minutes until soft. Add the spring onions and chives, followed by the baby spinach. Keep tossing in the pan until wilted and cooked. Place on a tray with kitchen paper to soak up any extra moisture.

To plate up, put some of the spinach mixture in the middle with some mushrooms around it. Place the fillet steak on top, followed by some onion jam. Just before you serve, place the tarragon butter on top.

You can serve this with fat fries (see p. 112), sweet potato wedges (see p. 155), or even a nice feta cheese and rocket salad on the side.

# WHOLE ROAST SEA BASS WITH RED CHILLI, ROASTED SWEET POTATO WEDGES & SPRING ONION & CAPER SALSA

SERVES 4

## INGREDIENTS

6 large sweet potatoes,
cut into large wedges
1 red chilli, chopped and seeded
1 tsp Cajun spice
4 tsp rapeseed oil
1 tsp chopped rosemary
4 cloves of garlic, chopped
4 whole sea bass (roughly 500g in total)
Butter
4 lime leaves

### LEMON & CHILLI BUTTER

100g butter
1 seeded red chilli, chopped
Zest of 1 lemon
Zest of 1 lime
2 cloves of garlic, chopped
1 tsp chopped parsley

### FRENCH DRESSING

1 tsp honey
1 tsp Dijon mustard
1 tsp white-wine vinegar
3 tsp olive oil

### SPRING ONION & CAPER SALSA

3 spring onions, finely sliced
6 cherry tomatoes, halved
12 black olives, pitted
2 tsp capers
1 tsp chopped coriander
1 tsp chopped basil
Juice and zest of 1 lemon

## METHOD

Preheat the oven to 170°C. Mix the sweet potato wedges with the chilli, Cajun spice, oil, rosemary and garlic. Make sure you give it a good mix and that all the potato has being coated well. Bake the potatoes in the oven for 30–35 minutes until nicely crispy.

For the lemon and chilli butter, make sure the butter is soft and then mix all the ingredients together.

Lay the sea bass on greased parchment paper, make a few slashes in both sides and rub melted butter onto the flesh. This will prevent the fish from sticking. Then stuff the fish cavities with the lime leaves. Roast in the oven, uncovered, for 20–25 minutes, until the skin is crispy and the fish is cooked.

For your French dressing, mix all the ingredients together and set aside.

The salsa is also nice and easy. Mix all the ingredients together, then combine with the French dressing.

To plate up, place the fish in the middle of the plate. Spoon the salsa over the top with the wedges on the side. You could also serve this with raita (see p. 66), which is beautiful with any kind of spicy food.

❋TIP:
Ask your fishmonger to give you four whole gutted sea bass and to remove the fins.

# THE BURKES' CHRISTMAS DINNER
# WITH ALL THE TRIMMINGS

I usually cook for Christmas, and, do you know what? I enjoy it: having all the family, the kids running around, and having a couple of beers making dinner. It's not often this happens in the kitchen! I do put on a good spread for Christmas dinner, but I don't do anything fancy – just your normal turkey dinner with all the trimmings. You might think you have a lot going on, but it's all about timing and doing some preparation the day before – the key is to plan ahead.

I personally use a turkey butterfly. This is boneless, with two large breasts, is easy to work with and there's no waste. It also stays nice and moist through the whole cooking process. The weight on a standard turkey is roughly between 5 and 6 kilogrammes. This will give you plenty of turkey for up to twelve main courses, with some left over for sandwiches.

SERVES 10–12

## INGREDIENTS

3kg spiced beef

4 carrots, sliced

4 sticks of celery, sliced

2 small white onions, sliced

8 sprigs of rosemary

5–6kg turkey butterfly (cut in two pieces: this will help it cook a bit faster)

Salt, to season

Olive oil

2.5kg bacon loin

### ROAST POTATOES

12 medium potatoes, peeled and halved

4 tsp rapeseed oil

1 tsp sea salt

1 tsp dried parsley

2 cloves of garlic, chopped

## METHOD

Place the spiced beef in the pot with half of the carrots, celery, onions and rosemary, and cover with water. Once it comes to the boil, leave to simmer for roughly 3½ hours – a slow braising.

Preheat the oven to 170°C. Place the rest of the vegetables in a deep roasting tray with the rest of the rosemary. Fill the tray three-quarters full of water – this will steam the turkey. Place the two turkey breasts on top. Rub the skin with salt and olive oil. Cover with parchment paper first, followed by tinfoil. Place in the oven and cook for 1¾ hours. Remove the tinfoil and parchment paper, and cook for another 1¼ hours to get the skin crispy. Keep checking that the water in the tray does not evaporate, and add more if needed. This keeps your turkey moist.

For the bacon, cook it the same way as in the recipe for cabbage and bacon on p. 108. Since this piece is bigger, you will need to cook for an extra 45 minutes.

For the roast potatoes, start by cooking the potatoes in salted water. Once they come to the boil, turn down the heat and leave

## CRANBERRY SAUCE

250g cranberries

Juice and zest of 1 orange

100ml orange juice

Pinch of cinnamon

Pinch of mixed spice

100g brown sugar

## POTATO STUFFING

150g butter

2 tsp dried mixed herbs

1 medium onion, diced

600g breadcrumbs (fresh)

150g mashed potato

## BRUSSEL SPROUTS

600g Brussel sprouts

10g hard butter

1 medium onion, diced

1 clove of garlic, chopped

1 tsp chopped parsley

## GRAVY

200ml red wine

1 shallot, diced

1 clove of garlic, chopped

1 sprig of thyme

1 sprig of rosemary

800ml chicken stock

3 tsp Knorr savoury gravy

## SIDES

Mash (see p. 108)

Honey-roast carrots (see p. 121)

Sprouting broccoli (see p. 141)

Spiced red cabbage (see pp. 120–1)

to simmer for 6 minutes. You want your potatoes still hard. Drain and place on an oven tray. Mix them with the oil, salt, parsley and garlic, and cook in the oven for 35–40 minutes until crispy and golden brown. Give the tray a shake every 15 minutes while cooking.

For the cranberry sauce, place all the ingredients into a pot and bring to the boil. Simmer for 15–20 minutes until the mixture forms into a jam. Leave to cool. This can be done a few days in advance and kept in the fridge.

For the potato stuffing, melt the butter with the herbs. Add the onion and cook without allowing the onion to colour. Once the onion is soft, add the breadcrumbs and cook for 1 minute. Then add the warm mash. Mix together and place into a bowl. This can also be done the day before.

Cook the sprouts in boiling water for 6 minutes until soft and tender. In a separate pot, melt the butter, then add the onion, garlic and parsley. Once the onion is soft, add the cooked sprouts and mix well. It's all about timing with the vegetables. Have them cooked 20 minutes before dinner and just keep them warm in the oven or in a pot covered with a lid.

For the gravy, reduce the red wine with the shallot, garlic and herbs by half. Add the chicken stock and any turkey stock you have left over. Reduce by two-thirds. Then thicken with Knorr savoury gravy. (If you want it thicker, add more powder.) Cook for a further 10 minutes, simmering gently. Then pass the sauce through a strainer. You should have a nice rich and silky sauce.

I carve the bacon first, then place the stuffing on top and lastly the turkey. The spiced beef is already sliced and left to the side. We put all the vegetables and potatoes in the middle of the table and everybody helps themselves.

✳ TIP:
Make sure you have enough gravy – it's used like soup at my table!

# CHRISTY'S CORNED-BEEF HASH WITH POACHED EGG, MUSTARD MAYO & ROCKET & TOMATO SALAD

In 2007 I leased the kitchen in Christy's Bar and Bistro in Arklow, County Wicklow, a great town with great people. Every Friday, corned beef was on the lunch menu. My local butcher, Larry Byrne, had the best corned beef. Larry was a great man for the banter and stories – just a lovely man. Every Friday, this dish went on as a lunch special, and boy it flew.

SERVES 4

## INGREDIENTS

4 large baking potatoes, peeled

40g butter, cubed

1kg cooked corned beef, shredded

1 tsp chopped chives

200g white cheddar, grated

2 tsp rapeseed oil

1 tsp distilled vinegar

4 eggs

### ROCKET & TOMATO SALAD

400g rocket leaves

8 cherry tomatoes, halved

1 red pepper, sliced

1 carrot, grated

2 tsp Roco's house dressing (see p. 78)

### MUSTARD MAYO

5 tsp mayonnaise

1 tsp Dijon mustard

2 tsp water

1 tsp chopped parsley

## METHOD

Boil the potatoes in salted water for 25 minutes until soft and cooked. Don't over-boil! Mash and add half the butter. Put in a bowl in the fridge. The potato must be cold.

When the mash is cold, mix with the corned beef, chives and cheese. With your hands make four round balls and press into equal-sized patties. Put on a tray and place in the fridge for at least 3 hours.

Preheat the oven to 180°C. Heat the rapeseed oil in a non-stick pan over a medium heat, then add the potato cakes. When they are golden brown underneath, turn over and add 20g of butter. When that side is golden brown, finish in the oven for 15–20 minutes.

For the salad, put the rocket on the plate first. Arrange the tomatoes on the side, and the pepper and carrot on top. You could also sprinkle some Parmesan on top.

For the mustard mayo, mix the mayonnaise and mustard together in a bowl, followed by the water and parsley. You want it to be wet and not too thick.

Heat a pot of water and add the vinegar. When the water is simmering, crack the eggs into the pot and turn the heat down to low. Leave the eggs to cook for 2–3 minutes. Remove them from the water with a slotted spoon.

Place your potato cake on the plate with the salad, add a poached egg on top, then spoon the mustard mayo over the egg. Serve the vinaigrette on the side.

✻TIP:
Never use salt in the water when poaching eggs as this will break the egg white.

DESSERTS

# GERRY'S CHOCOLATE POTS WITH SHORTBREAD BISCUITS

I was fifteen years old when I started in Rochestown Park Hotel. Not long before I started, a new executive chef was appointed: a big, tall, strong man and well spoken. You knew from day one that he was the boss. All the chefs were talking about him and about the places he had worked in, and that he was one of the first Irish chefs to receive a Michelin Star. Every move I made in my career was through his advice. My move to the Park Hotel in Kenmare, which really started my career, was thanks to him. From there I have never looked back.

People always ask me who inspired me in cooking. Most chefs would name a famous chef, but mine was a proud Irish man: Gerry Kirwan. He was a pure gentleman, flawless with words, a great teacher and a culinary genius in the kitchen. He was my hero in cooking. He was also my mentor and a friend I adored, who will not be forgotten.

SERVES 4–6

## INGREDIENTS

285ml cream

200g dark chocolate (55%)

2 egg yolks (from large eggs)

3 tsp brandy

20g butter

Whipped cream, berries and mint sprigs to garnish

SHORTBREAD BISCUITS (MAKES 8)

125g butter, soft

55g caster sugar

2g salt

180g plain flour

## METHOD

Heat the cream in a thick-bottomed saucepan, then add the chocolate. Remove from the heat and stir until melted.

Add in the egg yolks and brandy, then stir in the butter. Pour the mix into six espresso cups or shot glasses and leave to set in the fridge.

For the shortbread biscuits, mix the butter, sugar and salt in a bowl, then add the flour. Put onto a floured surface and knead, then shape into a ball. Leave to rest in the fridge for 3 hours.

Preheat oven to 170°C.

Gently roll the dough out on a floured surface. The pastry should be no more than 6 mm in thickness. Cut out eight biscuits using a cutter. Place on a tray lined with parchment paper and bake for 15 minutes, then place on a wire rack to cool.

Remove the chocolate pots from the fridge 20 minutes before serving. Garnish with whipped cream, berries and mint, and serve with shortbread biscuits on the side.

# THE MAHON KNICKERBOCKER GLORY

Born and raised in Mahon, I would not have had it that fancy, but Mam always gave it a good shot. Who does not like family fun on a hot day: ice cream and chocolate! My god-daughter Ashleigh helped me prepare the dish for the picture. Most supermarkets have good quality Irish ice creams, and some supermarkets use local Cork dairies for their ice cream, like Silver Pail and Happy Days ice cream.

SERVES 4

## INGREDIENTS

Lemon curd (see p. 179) or strawberry syrup

4 scoops of strawberry ice cream

120g strawberries, quartered

120g blueberries

4 scoops of chocolate ice cream

4 scoops of vanilla ice cream

300ml cream, whipped

37g bag of Maltesers

2 tsp sprinkles

2 tsp pink marshmallows

1 tsp nibbed almonds

4 Cadbury Flakes

1 tsp icing sugar

### CHOCOLATE SAUCE

250ml cream

60ml milk

250g dark chocolate drops

❋TIP:
Use knickerbocker glasses for serving if you can.

## METHOD

For the chocolate sauce, bring the cream and milk to the boil in a saucepan, then pour in the chocolate and whisk until it has melted. Chill in the fridge and microwave when needed.

Arrange the glasses. The lemon curd/strawberry syrup goes on the bottom. Then add one scoop of strawberry ice cream followed by some strawberries and blueberries.

Next, add one scoop of chocolate ice cream, again followed by berries, and then one scoop of vanilla ice cream.

Spoon a big dollop of cream on top, followed by Maltesers, sprinkles, pink marshmallows and almonds. Stick a flake in the centre, pour chocolate sauce on top and dust with icing sugar.

# BANANA TARTE TATIN WITH CRISPY ALMONDS & MASCARPONE CREAM

SERVES 4

## INGREDIENTS

5 bananas

100g butter

100g brown sugar

1 sheet of ready-made puff pastry (320g)

2 tsp flaked almonds

Icing sugar, to dust

MASCARPONE CREAM

100g mascarpone cheese

Juice and zest of 1 lime

1 tsp icing sugar

½ vanilla pod, seeds only

## METHOD

Preheat the oven to 190°C.

Peel the bananas and cut each one into five large chunks. This will give you twenty-five pieces.

In a small saucepan, melt the butter with the sugar over a low heat. Once melted, bring to the boil and leave to simmer for 3 minutes until golden brown, like a caramel. Pour the caramel into four 10 cm metal tart tins, leaving a little to finish the dish at the end. Arrange six pieces of banana on top of each.

Roll the puff pastry and pierce with a fork. Cut into circles to fit the tins, place on top of the banana and bake in the oven for 15–18 minutes until the pastry is golden brown. When the tarte Tatin is cooked, turn upside down on a plate. Watch your fingers as it will be very hot! There should be a nice glaze on the bananas.

For the mascarpone cream, mix all the ingredients together.

Roast the almonds for 3 minutes in the oven for a nice brown colour.

Sprinkle the toasted almonds over the banana, followed by a dusting of icing sugar and pour any caramel sauce you have left on top. Serve the mascarpone cream on the side.

♨VARIATION:
You can make all different tartes Tatin: apple, pear, peach, pineapple, and apricot. For harder fruits like apple and pear, cook the fruit in a syrup of water and sugar first, to soften.

# LEMON POSSET WITH CRISP HONEYCOMB & ROASTED STRAWBERRIES

A light refreshing dessert for the summer.

SERVES 4

## INGREDIENTS

### POSSET
300ml cream
100g caster sugar
Juice and zest of 1 lemon

### HONEYCOMB
75g caster sugar
2 tbsp golden syrup
1 tsp bicarbonate soda

### STRAWBERRIES
100g sugar
30g butter
400g medium-sized strawberries
Nutmeg

## METHOD

Mix the cream and sugar together and slowly bring to the boil. Allow to cook for 2 minutes. Turn off the heat and add the lemon juice and zest. Divide into four glasses and chill for at least 5 hours. Overnight would be even better.

To make the honeycomb, heat the sugar and golden syrup slowly in a saucepan until the sugar is dissolved and the syrup turns a deep amber colour. Stir the bicarbonate of soda into the mixture. It will bubble up. Pour onto a silicone sheet and leave to cool.

For the strawberries, add the sugar to a pan with a drop of water and cook until it reaches a light caramel colour. Add the butter, then the strawberries (with the green stem removed) and slowly cook for 3 minutes. The strawberries will not be soft but firm with a little bite. Leave to cool and add a pinch of nutmeg for some flavour.

To serve, place the cooled strawberries on top of the posset. Break the honeycomb into chunks, and place three pieces on each serving next to the strawberries.

❋TIP:
Add edible flowers and sprinkle with some black sesame seeds to really lift the dish's presentation.

# KAMIL'S MANGO CHEESECAKE WITH PASSION FRUIT

Kamil is my main man for the pastry in Rochestown Park Hotel. He's my BFG and is a big part of the success in our kitchen team. His mango cheesecake is a lovely, tasty, colourful and fresh-looking dessert.

SERVES 12

## INGREDIENTS

### CRUMB
170g digestive biscuits
80g granulated sugar
2 tsp cocoa powder
80g butter, melted

### FILLING
9 gelatine leaves
100ml cream
100g mango purée
1kg cream cheese
600g whipped cream
500g icing sugar

### PASSION FRUIT JELLY
4 gelatine leaves
200g passion fruit purée
170g sugar
130ml water

### TO GARNISH
Diced mango and strawberries
Fresh mint leaves
Raspberry sorbet

## METHOD

For your crumb, blitz the digestive biscuits in a food processor – don't make it too fine – remove and place into a bowl. Then add the sugar, cocoa powder and butter and mix well. Place in a cake tin (I use a 24 cm non-stick spring-form cake tin) and press your crumb down firmly. Leave to rest for a good hour if you can.

Soak your gelatine in 300ml of warm water. Warm your cream over a low heat, then add the strained gelatine leaves and whisk. The gelatine should dissolve into the liquid without any lumps. Then add your mango purée to the cream and whisk together.

In a bowl, mix the cream cheese, whipped cream and icing sugar together. Once mixed, add the mango cream and stir. Pour the mixture over your base, leaving 5 mm at the top of the cake tin for the jelly, and leave to set overnight in the fridge.

To make the passion fruit jelly, soak the gelatine in cold water for about 5 minutes until soft and pliable. Heat the purée, sugar and water in a pan. Add the drained gelatine and let it melt into the mix. Turn off the heat and allow the mixture to settle to room temperature. Make sure it's not too hot. Pour over the cheesecake and tilt the tin to spread evenly. Refrigerate for at least 6 hours until nice and firm.

To serve, dice some mango and strawberries. Place a spoonful next to a slice of cheesecake with some chopped mint leaves and serve with raspberry sorbet.

❊TIP:
The perfect cheesecake tin is important. I find a non-stick spring-form cake tin is best, but if you don't have one, you can also line the inside of a regular tin with parchment paper.

# MINI PAVLOVA WITH FRESH FRUIT & LEMON CURD

**SERVES 6**

## INGREDIENTS

4 egg whites

225g caster sugar

5g cornflour

1 tsp white-wine vinegar

1 vanilla pod

300ml cream

50g icing sugar

1 orange

2 kiwis

1 plum

¼ pineapple

2 passion fruit

Pomegranate seeds

1 punnet redcurrants

Mint leaves

### LEMON CURD

2 eggs

5 egg yolks

155g caster sugar

250g butter

Juice and zest of 2 lemons

## METHOD

Preheat the oven to 120°C.

Place the egg whites in a bowl and whisk until they reach a soft peak. Add the caster sugar a spoonful at a time, continuing to whisk all the while, until the mixture is thick and glossy. Follow with the cornflour and the vinegar, whisking again briefly to incorporate.

Spoon the meringue onto a baking sheet in six raised discs. Make sure you allow plenty of space between each one as they will expand. Bake for 1 hour until dry and crisp. Remove from the oven and cool on a wire rack.

For the lemon curd, cream the eggs, egg yolks and sugar. Melt the butter and add to the mixture, along with the lemon juice and zest. Whisk on a low heat until the mixture thickens, then simmer for 3 minutes. Leave to chill until needed.

For the whipped cream, cut the vanilla pod in half lengthways, scrape the seeds into the cream, then whisk with the icing sugar.

To plate up, put the curd on the bottom of the plate, with the meringue on top. Spoon on the whipped sweet cream and arrange your fruit on top with a sprig of fresh mint. You can slice or dice the fruit – it's totally up to you.

❋TIP:
If you don't have a vanilla pod, that's fine.
It will be sweet enough with the icing sugar in the cream.

# RASPBERRY MILLEFEUILLE

This is a nice, fluffy dessert – fresh raspberries between lemon curd, and the pastry is beautiful.

SERVES 4

## INGREDIENTS

2 ready-made puff pastry sheets (320g each)

3 tsp icing sugar

1 vanilla pod

500ml cream

4 tsp lemon curd (see p. 179)

200g raspberries

## METHOD

Preheat the oven to 200°C. Unroll the pastry and place on a non-stick baking tray. Dust with 1 teaspoon of icing sugar and bake in the oven for 15–20 minutes until the pastry is golden and glazed. Remove and leave to cool slightly on a wire rack.

For the cream, cut the vanilla pod lengthways and scrape the seeds into the cream. Whisk with 1 teaspoon of icing sugar until it forms soft peaks. Spoon the cream into a piping bag with a plain nozzle, and do the same with the lemon curd.

When the pastry has cooled, slice each sheet gently into six equal-sized lengths using a serrated knife; you should have 12 pieces in total.

To assemble each individual millefeuille, put a piece of pastry on the plate first, then a layer of cream. Add some raspberries, then pipe dots of lemon curd onto the raspberries. Add the second piece of puff pastry and repeat with the cream, raspberries and lemon curd. Finish with a top layer of pastry, and dust with the remaining icing sugar.

❄TIP:
Before putting the pastry on a serving plate, put a dot of cream on your plate to act as glue, so your pastry won't slide off.

# STICKY TOFFEE PUDDING WITH VANILLA ICE CREAM & TOFFEE SAUCE

SERVES 4

## INGREDIENTS

100g pitted dates
85g soft brown sugar
45g unsalted butter
1 egg, beaten
115g plain flour
1 tsp baking powder
1 tsp vanilla essence
Vanilla ice cream to serve

### TOFFEE SAUCE
150g demerara sugar
85g unsalted butter
4 tsp single cream
1 tsp black treacle
1 tsp golden syrup

## METHOD

Preheat the oven to 180°C. Grease 4 dariole moulds. If you don't have these to hand, you could also use a 24 cm square baking tray with parchment paper on the bottom and cut the pudding into square portions afterwards.

Put the dates into a pot, cover with water and bring to the boil. Simmer for 5 minutes until cooked. Once they are cooked, strain and blitz in a food processor or using a hand blender.

Cream together the soft brown sugar and the butter. Beat the egg into the creamed mixture and then add your flour slowly. Add the baking powder and vanilla essence and mix together, followed by the dates. Pour the mixture into your moulds and bake for 20–25 minutes until well risen.

For the toffee sauce, put the sugar, butter and cream into a pot. Bring to the boil over a medium heat, stirring all the time until the sugar has dissolved. Stir in the treacle and the golden syrup. Leave to bubble away on a high heat for 3 minutes, but make sure it does not burn. It should be a rich toffee colour.

Serve the pudding hot with the sauce and a scoop of local vanilla ice cream.

# CHOCOLATE & STRAWBERRY TRIFLE

This is nice and easy to prepare and can be made a day in advance. I have made a big bowl here, but you can make them individually as well. It's up to you.

SERVES 8–10

## INGREDIENTS

4 egg yolks

50g caster sugar

350ml double cream

600ml milk

1 vanilla pod

350g white chocolate drops

300g strawberry Swiss roll, sliced

20 large strawberries, halved

1 litre whipped cream

Icing sugar

Fresh edible flowers – amazing for colour

50g Cadbury Flake (two bars)

## METHOD

Cream the egg yolks and caster sugar together. Then whisk for 2 minutes until the mixture is pale, thick and creamy.

Combine the cream and milk in a pot. Cut the vanilla pod lengthways, scrape the seeds into the cream and bring to the boil. Pour the hot cream over the sugar and egg mixture. Put back into the pot and cook over a moderate heat. The custard is ready when it is thick enough to coat the back of your spoon.

Add the chocolate drops and stir until they're completely melted. Remove from the heat and allow to cool.

To assemble, first place the slices of the Swiss roll in the bottom and around the sides of the glass bowl, followed by a layer of strawberries. Pour the white chocolate custard on top followed by more strawberries and top with whipped cream. Garnish with icing sugar and edible flowers, and top with some crumbled chocolate flake.

VARIATIONS:
You could also make this with dark chocolate and raspberries. Follow the same method but change the white chocolate to dark chocolate, use a chocolate Swiss roll and, of course, raspberries instead of strawberries.

# APPLE MADEIRA WITH FRESH BERRIES & CARAMEL SAUCE

This is one of the first desserts I made, and I learned it from a French pastry chef, Yves, in the Park. Yves was a brilliant pastry chef, and this is a classic recipe. I'd say it is used all over Ireland by chefs who trained in the Park's kitchen.

 SERVES 12

## INGREDIENTS

Sweet pastry (see p. 188)

266g butter

266g sugar

4 eggs

½ tsp vanilla essence

266g plain flour

66g golden raisins

½ tsp ground cinnamon

2g bread soda

850g eating apple, cut in large dice

200g strawberries

150g blackberries

150g raspberries

150g redcurrants

### CARAMEL SAUCE

100g caster sugar

50ml water

50ml cream

25g salted butter

## METHOD

Preheat the oven to 150°C. Roll out the sweet pastry on a lightly floured surface and place into a greased 23 cm loose-bottomed tart tin. Leave to chill for 20 minutes.

Cream the butter and sugar until nice and fluffy. Add the eggs one at a time, mixing well, followed by the vanilla essence, flour, raisins, cinnamon and bread soda, and mix them all together. Fold the apple pieces into the mixture using your hands.

Fill the pastry case with your apple mixture. Cook for 1 hour and 20 minutes. The apples should be soft, and the cake should have a lovely brown colour. Insert a skewer to check that it's cooked – the skewer should come out clean.

To make the caramel sauce, combine the sugar and water in a small pan over a medium high heat. Allow to boil until the liquid turns a golden brown colour. Whisk in the cream followed by the butter to finish. If the sauce appears to be too thick, add a touch more cream to reach the consistency you want.

To serve, place the berries on top of a slice of cake, followed by your caramel sauce. And sure, why not finish it with a scoop of vanilla ice cream?

❋TIP:
Always serve this cake warm. Serving it cold does not do it justice!

# LEMON TART WITH FRESH RASPBERRIES & RASPBERRY PURÉE

SERVES 8

## INGREDIENTS

SWEET PASTRY
175g plain flour
85g unsalted butter
45g caster sugar
1 egg

RASPBERRY SAUCE
300g fresh raspberries
200g caster sugar

FILLING
5 eggs
200g caster sugar
Juice and zest of 4 lemons
200ml single cream

TO GARNISH
Icing sugar
Fresh raspberries

## METHOD

To make the sweet pastry, add the flour, butter and sugar to a food processor and pulse until it resembles breadcrumbs. Then add the egg and pulse until the pastry draws together into a ball. Roll out the pastry on a lightly floured surface, then place in a greased 23 cm loose-bottomed tart tin. Put in the fridge to chill for 20 minutes.

For the sauce, place the raspberries in a pot with the sugar and 100ml of cold water. Mix and heat gently until the sugar has dissolved. Bring to the boil, then reduce the heat and simmer for 5 minutes. The sauce should reduce by half and thicken. Pass through a sieve.

Preheat the oven to 190°C.

For the filling, beat the eggs and sugar together until combined. Then beat in the lemon zest and juice. Whisk in the cream and chill.

Line the pastry case with greaseproof paper, then fill with baking beans and bake blind for 12 minutes. Then remove the paper and baking beans and turn the temperature of the oven down to 150°C. Cook for a further 10 minutes until the base is crisp. Once the base has cooked, reduce the oven temperature to 120°C.

Pour the lemon filling into the pastry case. Be careful the filling doesn't spill over the edges. Bake for 20–25 minutes or until the tart is set. Remove from the oven and allow to cool.

Dust with icing sugar and serve it with fresh raspberries and the raspberry sauce.

# CHOCOLATE SOUFFLÉ WITH JAMESON ANGLAISE

SERVES 4

## INGREDIENTS

CRÈME ANGLAISE
150ml milk
350ml cream
½ vanilla pod
125g egg yolk
100g caster sugar
1 tsp Jameson

CHOCOLATE SOUFFLÉ
Butter for greasing
Caster sugar
210g dark chocolate (70%)
300ml milk
3 egg yolks
20g cornflour
50g caster sugar
6 egg whites
90g caster sugar
Icing sugar for dusting

## METHOD

Preheat the oven to 190°C.

For the crème anglaise, put the milk and cream in a pot over a medium heat. Scrape the seeds from the vanilla pod into the liquid and bring to the boil. Then remove from the heat.

Whisk the egg yolk and sugar in a bowl, then gradually add the hot cream mixture. Return the mixture to the heat and cook slowly until the custard thickens enough to coat the back of your spoon. Add the Jameson, then strain the anglaise and cool.

Brush four ramekins with melted butter and sprinkle with caster sugar.

Melt the chocolate in a bowl over a pan of simmering water.

Put the milk in another pot and bring to the boil. In a separate bowl, mix the egg yolks, cornflour and sugar together. Pour the boiling milk over this mixture and mix well. Put into the pot and back on the heat. Cook slowly for 3–4 minutes until it thickens. Remove from the heat, then add the melted chocolate, stirring slowly.

Whisk the egg whites to soft peaks or until they hold their shape. Add the sugar, 1 teaspoon at a time, whisking until you have a glossy and thick mixture. Gently fold this into the chocolate mixture. Fill the ramekins, wiping the rims clean. Cook in the oven for 10 minutes until risen with a slight wobble. Do not open the door while cooking as this may make them collapse.

When ready, sprinkle with icing sugar. Serve your crème anglaise on the side with a scoop of ice cream if you like.

# MIXED BERRY & PEAR CRUMBLE WITH CUSTARD

SERVES 4

## INGREDIENTS

### CRUMBLE
75g plain flour

50g butter

30g brown sugar

½ tsp ground cinnamon

25g porridge oats

25g walnuts, chopped

### FILLING
400g pears, peeled and sliced

Cinnamon to taste

20g caster sugar

15g butter

100g mixed berries (frozen or fresh)

### CUSTARD
175ml cream

175ml milk

1 vanilla pod, split

2 egg yolks

60g caster sugar

## METHOD

To make the crumble, place the flour in a bowl and rub in the butter until the mixture resembles fine breadcrumbs. Stir in the sugar, cinnamon, oats and chopped walnuts.

To make the filling, put the pears, cinnamon and half the sugar in a pot with the butter. Cook on a low heat, stirring often. When the sugar has dissolved and the pears have lightly softened and caramelised, add the berries and the remaining sugar. Cook for another 4 minutes, then put on a tray to cool.

Preheat the oven to 180°C. Place the fruit mixture into four small ovenproof dishes and scatter the crumble on top, covering all of the fruit. Cook in the oven for 15–20 minutes. The crumble should be a nice golden colour, and the filling should be bubbling up around the sides.

Meanwhile, for the custard, put the cream, milk and seeds from the vanilla pod into a pot and bring to the boil. Whisk the egg yolks and sugar together in a heatproof bowl until pale and smooth. Add the hot cream to the egg mixture, whisking to combine. It should be smooth and have thickened. Pass the custard through a sieve into a serving jug and serve alongside the hot crumble.

KIDS

# EGGY BREAD WITH BLUEBERRIES, BANANA & RASPBERRIES

SERVES 4

## INGREDIENTS

2 eggs

4 tsp milk

Pinch of cinnamon

2 tsp rapeseed oil

4 slices of bread, cut in half

1 punnet raspberries

1 punnet strawberries, quartered

2 small bananas, peeled and sliced

## METHOD

Whisk together the eggs and milk, and add a pinch of cinnamon.

Heat a non-stick frying pan over a medium heat, then add the oil.

Dip the bread into the egg mixture, making sure both sides are coated. Shake off any excess egg mix and place in the pan. Fry for 1½ minutes on each side, until cooked and golden brown.

Put the fried bread onto plates, with berries and banana on top. For an extra treat, add maple syrup. Enjoy!

❋TIP:
You can use any sort of bread, the thinner the better. If it's too thick, the egg won't soak in. At home we use O'Keeffe's, Cork's best bread!

# POACHED HADDOCK FILLET
# WITH MASH & MUSHY PEAS

This dish is great for baby bowls and also very good for freezing. Mix everything together once it's cooked, and blitz. If you usually use frozen fish, try using fresh – it's just better! Ask any good fishmonger and they will remove the fish bones for you.

 SERVES 4

## INGREDIENTS

4 large potatoes

500ml milk

1 bay leaf or 1 sprig of fresh thyme

400g haddock fillets (4 boned fillets)

1 tsp rapeseed oil

½ onion, diced

150g peas

100ml vegetable stock

## METHOD

The first job is to peel the potatoes. Cut them in half and cover with cold water. Bring the water to the boil, then simmer until cooked. This should take no more than 20 minutes.

Put the milk into a pot with the bay leaf or thyme and bring to the boil. Just as the milk is about to boil, add the fish and turn the heat to low. Allow the fish to simmer for 10–12 minutes without boiling. When it is cooked, remove and place on a tray, reserving the liquid. Double-check for fish bones by running your finger gently along the side of the fish.

Once the potatoes are cooked, strain and mash with a bit of the milk from the fish.

In another pot, add the rapeseed oil and sauté the onion without allowing it to colour. Add the peas followed by the hot stock. Cook for 2 minutes and then blitz.

Pop the fish on your plate first, followed by the peas and mash on the side.

❈TIP:
If you want to add more vegetables, add 50 grams of spinach to the mushy peas (they won't notice!) or chop up a carrot, which will bring some colour to the plate.

♨VARIATIONS:
You could use cod, smoked haddock or pollock instead of haddock. You could also cook salmon fillet, but use a fish stock, not milk.

# MINESTRONE SOUP WITH ANIMAL SHAPES

This dish is great for the kids. Nice, fast and full of vegetables.

SERVES 6—8

## INGREDIENTS

1 tsp rapeseed oil
½ onion, finely diced
1 carrot, diced
1 small courgette, diced
1 stick of celery, diced
1 yellow pepper, diced
1 small sweet potato, diced
400ml chopped tomatoes
400ml vegetable stock
20g peas
50g cooked pasta animal
shapes

## METHOD

Heat the rapeseed oil in a pan. Over a medium heat, sauté the onion, carrot, courgette, celery and yellow pepper.

Once the vegetables are halfway cooked, add the sweet potato, then the chopped tomatoes and stock.

Bring to the boil, then reduce to a low heat and allow to simmer for 20 minutes. Make sure all the vegetables are fully cooked – no child likes hard vegetables.

Add the peas and cooked pasta shapes and serve.

❋TIP:
This soup will keep in the fridge for up to two days,
or you can freeze it in portions.

♨VARIATION:
You could also add fish, beef, chicken or ham,
but these need to be cooked first.

# PENNE BOLOGNESE

**SERVES 4–6**

## INGREDIENTS

Rapeseed oil

300g lean mince

½ onion, finely chopped

1 carrot, finely chopped

1 red pepper, finely chopped

1 stick of celery, finely chopped

½ courgette, finely chopped

1 tsp chopped spinach leaves

6 mushrooms, chopped

1 tsp tomato paste

200g passata

200g penne pasta

Light red cheddar, grated

## METHOD

Heat a little oil in a large saucepan and fry your mince until brown all over.

Once the meat has coloured, add the onion, carrot, red pepper, celery, courgette, spinach and mushrooms, and allow to cook slowly for 5 minutes.

Stir in the tomato paste, followed by the passata and slowly cook for 15–20 minutes.

Bring a large pot of salted water to the boil, then cook the penne pasta for 10–12 minutes. It's a good idea to add 1 teaspoon of rapeseed oil to your boiling water to prevent the penne from sticking together.

When the pasta is cooked, strain and put into a bowl. Ladle your Bolognese sauce on top and sprinkle with some grated cheddar cheese. Garlic bread won't go astray with this dish!

# CORKONIAN BEEF & VEGETABLE CASSEROLE

SERVES 6–8

## INGREDIENTS

1 tbsp rapeseed oil

400g diced beef

1 onion, diced

1 stick of celery, diced

2 carrots, diced

1 small turnip, diced

1 sprig of thyme, chopped

2 tsp tomato paste

1 tsp plain flour

400ml beef stock (made with 2 stock cubes)

2 large baking potatoes, diced

## METHOD

Preheat the oven to 160°C.

Heat a large casserole dish over a medium heat, add the rapeseed oil and then add the beef – you want to seal the meat all over.

When the beef is brown, add the diced onion, celery, carrots, turnip and thyme, and cook for 4 more minutes. You want to release the flavours from the vegetables.

Add the tomato paste followed by the flour and beef stock. If your child is allergic to gluten, you can leave out the flour and add a third potato.

Bring the sauce to the boil, then add the potatoes. Put on the lid and put it into the oven to cook for 2 hours 30 minutes, or until the meat is tender. After this length of time you should have a beautiful casserole full of flavour – a nice hearty stew for the kids.

❋TIP:
You can make this in bigger batches and freeze, as it freezes really well.

# TURKEY SLIDERS WITH BABY GEM & CHERRY-TOMATO KETCHUP

SERVES 8

## INGREDIENTS

400g turkey mince

50g breadcrumbs

1 egg, beaten

1 tsp rapeseed oil

8 mini burger buns

1 small baby gem lettuce

KETCHUP

½ red onion, diced

1 tsp rapeseed oil

200g cherry tomatoes, halved

1 sprig of thyme, chopped

1 tsp white-wine vinegar

1 tsp sugar

4 tsp tomato juice

## METHOD

For the ketchup, sauté the onion over a medium heat in 1 teaspoon of rapeseed oil, without allowing it to colour. Add the tomatoes and thyme and allow to cook for another 3 minutes.

Add the white-wine vinegar, sugar and tomato juice and allow to cook slowly for 20 minutes until it looks like a chutney. Then blitz to a fine purée. Allow to cool.

To make the turkey sliders, mix the turkey mince, breadcrumbs and egg. Divide the mixture into eight small patties and place in the fridge for 30 minutes to rest. Preheat the oven to 170°C.

Heat a large pan and add 1 teaspoon of rapeseed oil. When good and hot, seal the burgers on both sides and then put in the oven for 10 minutes until cooked.

Then grill your burger buns and put one leaf of baby gem on top, followed by the turkey burger and the ketchup. Serve with sweet potato fries on the side – yummy!

VARIATION:
Replace the turkey mince with beef.

# CHOCOLATE NESTS WITH POPPING CANDY

🍴 SERVES 6

## INGREDIENTS

250g milk chocolate

Zest of 2 oranges

100g crème fraîche

200g cornflakes (crushed)

20g popping candy

White chocolate drops for sprinkles

## METHOD

Line a square brownie tray, 21 × 30 cm, with baking paper.

Place the chocolate in a bowl over a pan of simmering water until melted. Stir in the orange zest and crème fraîche.

Crush the cornflakes with your hands and fold into the chocolate. Allow to cool, then stir in the popping candy.

Using a pallet knife, spread evenly on the tray. Try to make sure the mixture is smooth on top. With a spoon, sprinkle white chocolate drops on top and leave to set in the fridge for 3 hours.

To serve, cut in squares.

♨VARIATIONS:
Try changing-up the recipe and use Rice Krispies instead of cornflakes and white chocolate instead of milk.

# STRAWBERRY LOLLIPOPS

Ψ SERVES 12

## INGREDIENTS

100ml cream
100g fresh strawberry purée
Juice of ½ lime
200g white chocolate
25g butter

TO DECORATE
100g melted chocolate
2 tsp sprinkles

## METHOD

Put the cream, strawberry purée and lime juice in a pot and heat. Once it starts to boil, whisk in your chocolate followed by your butter. When it is all melted and combined, remove from the heat. Pour into a bowl and allow to cool. Then cover with cling film and chill overnight.

Using an ice-cream scoop, make balls from the chilled mixture. If you have a Parisian scoop great, if not a normal scoop is fine. You should get twelve round balls. Put the balls in the fridge for 1 hour.

Insert lollipops sticks into the balls, then dip them into the melted chocolate and then into the sprinkles.

♨ VARIATIONS:
You could use different fruit purées, like raspberry
or blackcurrant.

# FRESH FRUIT LOLLIES

These are simple but brilliant and are great not only for getting fresh fruit into your kids but also for teething. On many nights the ice lollies have been brought out to numb poor gums.

 SERVES 4–6

## INGREDIENTS

## METHOD

STRAWBERRY & RASPBERRY
LOLLIES

300g strawberries

300g raspberries

PINEAPPLE & MANGO
LOLLIES

1 pineapple, cut into chunks

2 medium mangos, cut into
chunks

Blend the fruit until smooth. Pass the mixture through a strainer, then pour into your ice-lolly moulds.

Freeze overnight.

REDCURRANT & RASPBERRY
LOLLIES

100g raspberries

100g redcurrants

180g full-fat yoghurt

Blend the fruit until smooth. Pass the mixture through a strainer into a bowl.

Fold in the yoghurt, then pour into your ice-lolly moulds.

Freeze overnight.

PASSION FRUIT & MANGO
LOLLIES

2 medium mangos, cut into
chunks

1 passion fruit

¼ pineapple, finely diced

180g full-fat yoghurt

Blend the mango and flesh of the passion fruit until smooth. Pass the mixture through a strainer into a bowl.

Mix the diced pineapple with the fruit purée. Fold in the yoghurt and mix together.

Pour into your ice-lolly moulds and freeze overnight.

# FAIRY CUPCAKES

**SERVES 12**

## INGREDIENTS

150g butter
150g caster sugar
150g plain flour
½ tsp baking powder
3 eggs

### BUTTERCREAM
150g soft butter
150g icing sugar
75g white chocolate, melted
Food colouring of your choice

### TOPPINGS
Maltesers
Sprinkles

## METHOD

Preheat the oven to 170°C. Line a cupcake tin with 12 coloured cupcake paper cases.

In a mixing bowl, cream the butter and sugar until light and creamy. Add the flour and baking powder, then fold in the eggs one by one to form a smooth batter.

Spoon the batter into the paper cases, just above halfway up, as they will rise when cooking. Bake in the oven for 12–15 minutes until lightly browned. Remove from the tin and cool.

For the buttercream, mix the butter and sugar until nice and fluffy, then add the melted white chocolate. Separate this into two equal batches of icing. Add a drop of your food colouring into one batch for colour, and whisk together. Place both batches of icing into separate bags with a star nozzle.

Pipe the different buttercreams onto the cupcakes and decorate with sprinkles and Maltesers. As you can see, Liam really enjoyed his blue cupcake on his first birthday!

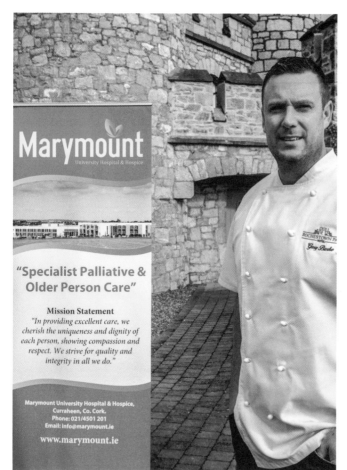

# ACKNOWLEDGEMENTS

Thank you for the kind gesture you've just made on behalf of the families, friends and staff of Marymount Hospice. The money raised from this cookbook will help Marymount continue to offer the support and services it provides to so many Cork families. Its safe, calm environment allows families to share those last precious moments with their loved ones, and its renowned comfort and care is appreciated by the entire community.

The concept for the book was devised with Rochestown Park back in 2017 and what a journey we have had in delivering this book to you and to Marymount. Steve Cox, I could not have done this special book without your tireless work and also without your putting up with me! Thank you.

We could not have brought this project to reality without the support of the hotel and our food suppliers. Sincere thanks to:

Rochestown Park Hotel

Kitchen Team RPH

Quigley Meats

All Fresh Fruit and Veg

Gulfstream Kenmare

P. O'Connell Butchers

Ballycotton Seafood

Clona Dairies

Meadow Fresh

Higgins & Co. Catering

Cyril Murphy Refrigeration

Cork Bar & Catering

John Giltsharp

Musgraves, Cork

A special thank you to Rochestown Park Hotel, which has backed every element of this project as part of the hotel's thirtieth anniversary, and Fionn Mulvey for taking the perfect pictures.

And last but not least my incredible wife, Paula, whose vision and support drives me on. Also my beautiful kids, Maisie and Liam.

# INDEX

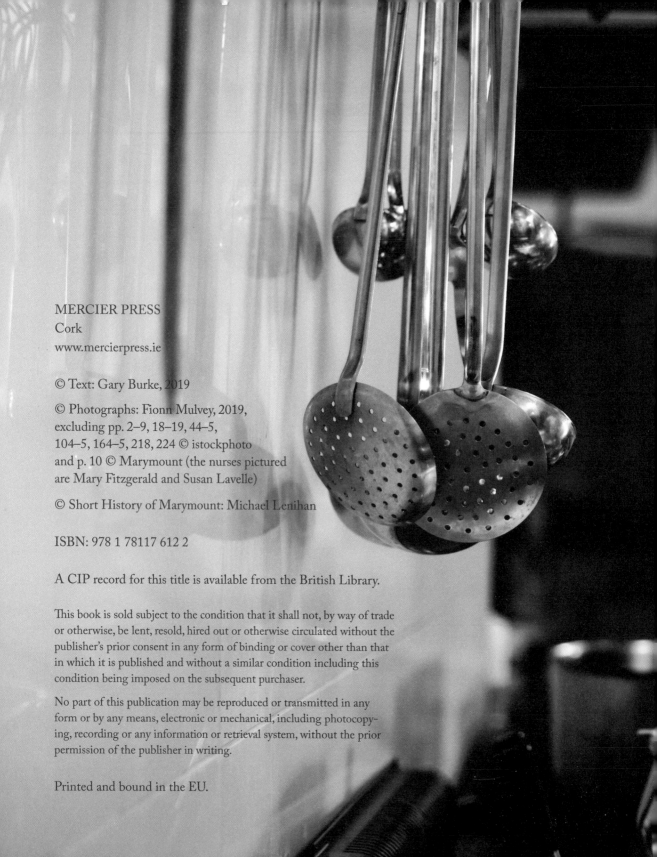

MERCIER PRESS
Cork
www.mercierpress.ie

© Text: Gary Burke, 2019

© Photographs: Fionn Mulvey, 2019,
excluding pp. 2–9, 18–19, 44–5,
104–5, 164–5, 218, 224 © istockphoto
and p. 10 © Marymount (the nurses pictured
are Mary Fitzgerald and Susan Lavelle)

© Short History of Marymount: Michael Lenihan

ISBN: 978 1 78117 612 2

A CIP record for this title is available from the British Library.

Printed and bound in the EU.